Apply Yourself

English for Job Search Success

Lisa Johnson

Lynn Levey

Elizabeth Chafcouloff

Longman

We would like to dedicate this book to all the refugees and immigrants here and around the world who have made a difficult journey in anticipation of building a new and better life. We hope this book can help them on their quest.

Acknowledgments

First we would like to thank our partners: Terri Massin, Andrew Blasky, and Jeffrey Kao, and Lynn's children: Jesse Levey and Maraya Massin-Levey, whose understanding and enthusiastic support made this project possible. In particular, we would like to thank Terri for suggesting the title of the book, Terri and Andrew for their helpful editorial comments, Jesse and Jeffrey for their assistance in developing tapes for field testing, and Maraya for her patience and encouragement.

We initially conceived of this project while teaching in the Vocational ESL program at Jewish Vocational Service (JVS) in San Francisco. Special thanks go to JVS and our colleagues there, especially Mary Claycomb, Alex Scott, and Maw Win for giving us valuable insight on earlier versions of this material.

We would like to thank our reviewers for their time and expertise: Myra Baum, NYC Public Schools; Linda Cobb, Private Industry Council; Patricia DeHesus-Lopez, Texas A & M University; Sally Gearhart, Santa Rosa Junior College; Margie Glasier, Merced College; Janet Langon, New York Association for New Americans (NYANA); Mary Nance-Tager, LaGuardia Community College; Alice Rosenthal, City College of San Francisco; Maria Rousseau, Lindsey Hopkins Technical Education Center; Chris Shaw, Career Resources Development Center; and Carl Wells, Jobtrack.

We would also like to express our appreciation to the following people for their help: John Rosenberg, Sonia Tuchinsky, Mary Kay Hunyady, Joan Hopkins, Liz Fisher, Yelena Zimon, Frank Duhl, Alexsis Beach, Noelle Hanrahan, Jennifer Beach, David Block, Bob Wells, Anchalee Kurutach, Seng Thongvanh, Adinah Barnett, Damon Kendall, Vicki Legion, Nicole Wendell, Robert Griffiths, Glen Claycomb, Janice Wood, and Terri Moses.

Finally, we are grateful to our students, who have inspired us and guided our efforts. Their feedback and innovative ideas were critical to the development of this book.

Text credit: pages 144–145 Ross Stores, Inc.

Apply Yourself: English for Job Search Success

Pearson Education, 10 Bank Street, White Plains, NY 10606

Editorial Director: Joanne Dresner
Senior Acquisitions Editor: Anne Boynton-Trigg
Development Editor: Karen Davy
Production Editor: Liza Pleva
Text Design: Curt Belshe
Electronic Production Coordinator: Kim Teixeira
Cover Design: Joseph DePinho
Interior Art: Shelly Matheis

Library of Congress Cataloging-in-Publication Data
Johnson, Lisa, 1960–
    Apply Yourself: English for job search success/Lisa Johnson, Lynn Levey, Elizabeth Chafcouloff.
        p.   cm.
    ISBN 0–201–87684–1
    1. English language—textbooks for foreign speakers.
2. Vocational guidance—Problems, exercises, etc. 3. Job hunting—Problems, exercises, etc. 4. Readers—Vocational Guidance.
5. Readers—Job hunting. I. Levey, Lynn. II Chafcouloff, Elizabeth. III. Title
PE1128.J586 1996
428.2'4—dc 20   95—53997
                                                CIP

15 16 17 18 V012 14 13 12 11

Contents

Introduction

The job search in North America is not a simple, straightforward process; it has become a complicated system full of formulaic language and specific rules to follow. If job seekers are often daunted by this system, job seekers with limited English proficiency (LEP) are especially at a disadvantage.

LEP job seekers often lack the necessary language skills to access job-search books and training materials or to perform basic job-search tasks. In addition, LEP job seekers are usually unfamiliar with cultural assumptions underlying the job search in North America. Typically, these conditions undermine self-confidence and make success difficult to achieve.

Apply Yourself was created for these LEP job seekers, particularly for those at a high-beginning or intermediate level of English. By providing them with practice in job-search skills within a classroom setting, *Apply Yourself* aims to increase their potential for job-search success and to raise their confidence level significantly.

Apply Yourself leads LEP learners step by step from early and simple job-search tasks through later and more complex tasks. Language skill-building—with a special emphasis on listening, speaking, and vocabulary—is integrated throughout *Apply Yourself,* as is the teaching of job-search cultural concepts. The presentation of both language and concepts is carefully sequenced to correspond to the growing complexity of the job-search tasks introduced, and important material is continually recycled.

TEACHING APPROACH

Studying job-search skills can be anxiety provoking even for the most motivated learner. At the same time, the detailed content of a job-search course can be dry and dense. For these reasons, *Apply Yourself* includes a wide variety of activities to keep learners involved and interested.

Teachers need not use nor complete every exercise. It is more important to keep the energy level of the classroom high by promoting learner-to-learner interaction, and encouraging learners to change partners or groups often. Games and performance-based tasks appearing at the end of units should not be omitted; games provide needed levity and performance-based tasks offer learners a crucial bridge between the classroom and the real world.

Teachers can add interest and invaluable feedback by audiotaping and videotaping the class. Learners can be audiotaped, for example, when practicing telephone conversations with receptionists or managers. When body language is important, videotaping supplies visual feedback; learners can be videotaped practicing interview questions, for example, or while role playing introducing themselves to an employer.

The class can listen to or watch these taped interactions and critique them with the teacher.

It is a good idea to add some job-search motivational activities to the class. For example, the teacher can set up a "job-lead" bulletin board where students and the teacher can post information about job openings from want ads, job listings, or networking. The teacher can also put up a chart where the class records its job-search steps, such as telephone calls made, interviews attended, and applications filled out.

OVERVIEW OF THE TEXTBOOK

Apply Yourself treats four basic job-search themes in eight units. Units 1 and 2 emphasize general preparation for the job search and the most common job-search strategies; Units 3 and 4 teach telephone skills necessary for the job search; Units 5 and 6 present job applications, resumes, and cover letters; and Units 7 and 8 focus on the job interview and interview follow-up.

Units 1 through 4 are designed to be used in order. Even if time constraints mean that the teacher cannot introduce or exploit all of the exercises, the key concepts and language should be introduced sequentially. Units 5 and 6 are somewhat less interactive. We suggest that these units be taught in conjunction with Units 7 and 8.

The *Apply Yourself* textbook is accompanied by one 90-minute audiocassette tape. A tapescript is included at the end of the textbook.

DESCRIPTION OF EXERCISE TYPES AND SUGGESTIONS FOR USE

What Do You Think?

Students preview the subject matter of each unit in a brainstorming/discussion format. Questions encourage students to share what they already know and stimulate their curiosity to learn more. This activity sets up a friendly and informal atmosphere in the classroom, and helps the teacher to assess the language level and cultural sophistication of students.

What Do You Think? can be used as a small-group activity with summations by the whole class or as a teacher-guided, whole-class discussion.

Teaching Texts

Key concepts are presented in paragraph form. Students can read the texts for homework, or the teacher can simply use the texts as references for classroom presentation. In either case, students benefit most when asked to participate. Teachers should avoid simply reading the texts to the students.

"How To" Boxes

Step-by-step lists of functions or "how to's" associated with a particular job-search task appear in boxes following presentations of concepts. Students use these function lists as reference points for exercises immediately following.

Words for Success

LEP students are often overwhelmed by the large amount of specific job-search vocabulary that needs to be understood and produced. In *Apply Yourself*, this vocabulary is presented in meaningful contexts followed by exercises for immediate reinforcement. Vocabulary is continually recycled throughout the book, so that students have ample opportunity to revisit key words and expressions.

A distinction is made between passive and active vocabulary, since students usually need to understand—through listening or reading—a great many more words and expressions than they need to produce through speaking. For example, listening exercises use vocabulary that students will hear but will not necessarily need to produce. Words for Success, however, focuses primarily on vocabulary that students will need to use during their job search. Therefore, students using *Apply Yourself* spend most of their valuable time verbalizing language that they will actually need to use in the real world.

Vocabulary exercises are simple and straightforward, including matching, fill-in, or multiple choice. Exercises can be assigned as homework or can be done in class in pairs or small groups.

Language Focus

Occasionally language routines present particular difficulties, or involve grammar that may be unfamiliar to low-level students. In these cases, language focus exercises break the language down and offer controlled practice.

Language Focus exercises are highly structured and are best completed in pairs of students so that learners gain the necessary practical fluency to put these routines into use.

Listening

Listening development is particularly emphasized in *Apply Yourself* because the job search typically entails understanding a great deal of verbal communication. LEP job seekers must be able to understand information given to them by receptionists and employers, and they must be able to understand and respond to a large number of questions.

Generally, three types of listening tasks develop a variety of skills and strategies: listening for the main idea, listening for details, and cloze listening. Some listening exercises preview important concepts and develop prediction strategies, while more focused exercises reinforce language and vocabulary already practiced.

Students may need to hear the taped sections several times in order to complete the exercises. During later listenings, the teacher may want to stop the tape frequently, eliciting responses from the class after each pause.

Student-to-student interaction can be incorporated into listening exercises by asking students to compare their answers before the teacher offers corrections.

Pair Work

Pair Work activities are generally of two types: structured practice and information gap. Structured practice activities give students the opportunity to rehearse language routines, or to repeat key vocabulary in a conversational context.

Information gap activities provide a bridge between structured practice and real communication as students take turns speaking and listening. Students are looking at different guidelines or information and must pay close attention to what is being said, asking for clarification and confirmation when necessary.

Pair work can be most useful when learners change partners frequently. This creates a lively classroom atmosphere and gives learners maximum feedback on their language performance.

Team Work

Team Work consists of small-group cooperative learning activities in which students analyze situations and solve problems associated with the job search. As they discuss, students draw upon earlier brainstorming sessions for ideas and make use of language routines and vocabulary learned in previous exercises. In addition to practicing language in a less structured context, students also develop team work skills needed for the workplace. They learn to negotiate, to ask for repetition and clarification, and to offer mutual support.

Teamwork groups are ideally composed of three or four students.

On Your Own

In these exercises, students work alone to sum up concepts and language practiced in earlier exercises. On Your Own tasks usually involve written reinforcement and can be done for homework or in class.

Culture Notes

Culture Notes appear once or twice per unit. Each set of Culture Notes exposes students to one aspect of the cultural assumptions peculiar to the job search in North America. Often presented as a list of "shoulds" and "shouldn'ts," Culture Notes deepen students' understanding of cross-cultural differences, prepare them for the expectations of the job search, and help them to avoid cultural mistakes.

Culture notes are always followed by discussion questions and/or structured exercises appropriate for small groups or pair work.

Role Play

Appearing near the end of most units, Role Plays give students a last classroom opportunity to practice the language and behavior they have learned so far. Students are given bare-bones guidance, and asked to create situations which simulate real-life job-search tasks. Because of the loosely structured nature of these activities, students must really hone their listening and speaking skills in order to participate. There is also ample room for exploration and creativity, enabling students to discover their strengths and the areas in which they need to improve.

Many of the Role Plays are designed for pair work, although some are suggested as small group activities, depending on the tasks to be accomplished in a particular unit.

Apply Yourself

These activities send students into an active job search in the real world. They are asked to make contact with members of their community and to put into practice the job-search skills they have learned in the classroom. They must then report back to classmates and teacher, and keep records of their progress.

Apply Yourself activities take place outside of class. Students usually accomplish these tasks individually, although students may go out in pairs for moral support, provided that the actual community contact is made on an individual basis.

Games for Review

Games, which appear at the very end of each unit, give learners the opportunity to synthesize what they have learned in a relaxed and friendly competition with their classmates. The games at the end of the even-numbered units review the paired units (units 1 and 2, 3 and 4, 5 and 6, 7 and 8). The games at the end of the odd-numbered units review only one unit.

GAME INSTRUCTIONS

Sentence and Question Scramble

Materials
One game for each group

Object
Each group makes as many sentences as possible, using the words in the boxes.

Play
1. Play in small groups.
2. Choose one person in each group to write the sentences.
3. Look at the words in the boxes.
4. Make as many sentences as possible, using the words in the boxes.
5. The sentences must be grammatically correct.
6. It is possible to use each word many times. Do not use any words that are not in boxes.
7. The playing time is five minutes for each part of the game.

Checking in
At the end of the activity, see how many sentences each group made and write the sentences on the board. Check for errors with the whole class. The group with the most correct sentences wins.

Unit 3 (Exercise 30, pages 84 and 85)
Context: A job applicant is calling about a job and talking to the receptionist.

Some Possible Answers
Unit 3, Part A:

1. My name is Olivia Peralta.
2. I'm calling about the job as a cook.
3. I saw your ad in the *Daily News*.
4. Olivia Peralta told me that you have a job opening.
5. I'm interested in the job as a cook.
6. My telephone number is 641-9909.
7. I'm Olivia Peralta.

Unit 3, Part B:

1. May I leave a message, please?
2. Could you tell me the manager's name, please?
3. Could you spell that, please?
4. Could you spell the manager's name, please?
5. Please tell the manager that I called.
6. Could you take a message, please?
7. Is that Mr. or Ms.?
8. May I have the manager's name, please?
9. Could I have the manager's name, please?
10. Could I leave a message, please?
11. Could you tell the manager that I called, please?

Unit 7 (Exercise 23, page 177)
Context: A job applicant is answering basic interview questions.

Some Possible Answers
Unit 7:

1. I prefer full-time, but I'm flexible.
2. I prefer part-time, but I'm flexible.
3. I can start immediately.
4. I can start Monday.
5. I can work anytime.
6. I can work any shift.
7. I'd like the salary you usually pay for this position.
8. I'm open.
9. I prefer full-time, but I can work part-time.
10. I prefer part-time, but I can work full-time.

11. I'd like part-time work.
12. I'd like full-time work.
13. I'm flexible.
14. I can work part-time, but I prefer to work full-time.
15. I can work full-time, but I prefer to work part-time.
16. I can work part-time, but I prefer full-time work.
17. I can work full-time, but I prefer part-time work.
18. I'd like to work full-time.
19. I'd like to work part-time.
20. I'd like full-time work.
21. I'd like part-time work.

Board Games

Materials
One game board and one die or coin for every four players. (If you use a coin instead of a die, heads can be 1 and tails can be 2. This will make the game go slower and will give students more opportunities to answer most of the questions.)

One marker for each player. (Students can use a penny, a ring, a colored piece of paper, etc.)

Object
Move from *Start* to *Winner* by performing language tasks correctly.

Play
1. Play in small groups.
2. Put markers in the *Start* circle.

The first player rolls the die or flips the coin and moves the appropriate number of spaces in the direction of the arrows. She/he then attempts to perform the **language task*** written on the space.

If the other players decide that his/her answer is correct, the player remains on the space. If the answer is incorrect, the player moves back to the space the player was on before the roll. Then the second player rolls the die or flips the coin.

Play continues until all the players have entered the *Winner* space in the center of the board.

Unit 4 (Exercise 24, page 103)
Telephone Board Game

☆ The sentence is incorrect. There is one mistake. Correct the sentence.

= What is another way to say the sentence? Rephrase the sentence.

☺ The sentence is impolite. Make a polite sentence.

Unit 8 (Exercise 49, page 209)
Interview Board Game

☒ Discuss this job-search idea.

? Answer the interview question.

Teacher's Role
The instructor acts as a facilitator by moving from group to group, answering questions, and settling disputes.

"Go Fish" Card Game

Materials
The teacher will write the words or expressions from the squares onto index cards or colored paper, making one set for each pair or group. The teacher gives each pair or group one set of cards.

Object
Match the cards that have the same meaning. Collect as many cards as possible.

Play
1. Play in pairs or groups of three.
2. Give each group member five cards.
3. Put the remainder of the cards on the table, face down.

The first player chooses one card in his/her hand and reads the card to the other people in his/her group to see if anyone has a match. If there is a match, the first player takes the card, puts it down with its match, and goes again. This continues until there is no match. Then the first player picks a card from the deck, and the next player goes.

Play continues until all the cards are matched. The students count the cards (points) they have. The student with the most points wins.

Unit 5 (Exercise 21, page 124)

***Language tasks:** There are five types of language tasks. A symbol in each space identifies the task type.

UNIT 1

Getting Ready for Your Job Search

WHAT DO YOU THINK?

Discuss these questions with your classmates.

1. Are you working now?
   Did you have a job in your country?
   If you worked, what kind of job did you have?

2. How do people find jobs in your country?
   If you had a job in your country, how did you find your job?

3. What do you know about finding a job in this country?
   If you have (or had) a job here, how did you find your job?
   If you have friends who are working here, how did they find their jobs?

4. What kind of job are you looking for now?
   Why are you looking for that kind of job?
   What kind of job do you want to have five years from now?

5. What did you need to think about and prepare before you looked for a job in your country?
   Do you think that these things are the same or different in this country?

In this unit, you will:

- Talk about what kind of job you want to look for.

- Learn what you need to do before you look for a job.

- Think about your personal qualities (what kind of person you are).

- Think about your skills (what you can do).

- Find out how people in North America look for jobs.

YOUR JOB GOAL

Before you look for a job, it is very important to think about your **job goal**. What kind of job do you want? What kind of job can you do?

Sometimes you cannot find the job that you really want. Before you can do that job, you may need to study more or you may need more experience. When people cannot find the job they want, they often look for entry-level jobs—beginning jobs where you do not need many special skills.

An entry-level job can help you in the future. First, you can improve your

English. You can also get experience in North America and learn about the work culture in North America. Finally, you can learn skills that you can use in another job.

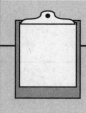

HOW TO FIND YOUR JOB GOAL

There are two types of job goals:

- **Short-term goal:** What job can you do now?
- **Long-term goal:** What kind of job do you want in the future? What kind of job do you want in five years?

To find your short-term and your long-term job goals, you need to think about who you are and about what you can do. You need to think about:

- Your **personal qualities**: Are you a hard worker? Are you good with numbers?
- Your **skills**: Can you use a computer? Can you work with children? Can you drive? Can you use any machines?

After you think about your job goals, your personal qualities, and your skills, write down this information. For some jobs, you need to write:

- A **resume**: A one-page, typed document about your skills and personal qualities, your past jobs, and your education. You will learn more about this in Unit 6.

🎧 1 LISTENING

Alex and his friend are talking about Alex's goals, personal qualities, and skills. Read the questions. Then listen to the conversation. Circle the correct letter or letters.

1. What are Alex's personal qualities?
    a. He can use a computer.
    b. He can cook.
    c. He works well with people.
    d. He is a fast learner.

2. What are Alex's work skills?
    a. He is a fast learner.
    b. He can use a computer.
    c. He can help sick people.
    d. He is friendly.

3. What was Alex's past job?
    a. He was a painter.
    b. He was a nurse.
    c. He used a computer.
    d. He was a cook.

4. What is Alex's long-term goal?
    a. He wants to work in a big company.
    b. He wants to be a doctor.
    c. He wants to work with computers.
    d. He wants to be a nurse.

5. What is Alex's short-term goal?
    a. He wants to work in a restaurant.
    b. He wants to help sick people in their homes.
    c. He wants to be a nurse.
    d. He wants to work with computers.

6. What will Alex write about in his resume?
    a. his job goal
    b. his family
    c. his skills and personal qualities
    d. his education and past jobs

Before you look for a job

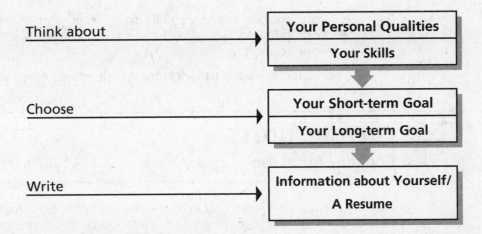

Think about ⟶ | Your Personal Qualities |
| Your Skills |

Choose ⟶ | Your Short-term Goal |
| Your Long-term Goal |

Write ⟶ | Information about Yourself/ |
| A Resume |

2 WORDS FOR SUCCESS

Match the phrases on the left with the sentences on the right. Write the correct number on each line. You can use each number more than once.

1. Skill
2. Personal quality
3. Short-term goal
4. Long-term goal

___ Now I want to be a waitress.

<u>1</u> I can cook.

___ I am a hard worker.

___ I want to be a nurse in five years.

___ I can fix cars.

___ I'm organized.

LANGUAGE FOCUS
Questions to Ask When You Don't Understand

When you do not understand what people are saying, it is good to ask questions. You need to ask polite questions.

When you want people to repeat what they said, you can say:

- Excuse me?
- Could you repeat that, please?

When people are talking very fast, you can say:

- Could you speak more slowly, please?

When you do not understand a word or some words, you can say:

- Could you say that in other words?
- What does _____ mean?

3   PAIR WORK

Tell your partner a story about:

- your hobbies (what you like to do in your free time).
- your family.
- your country.

Then listen to your partner's story. Ask questions when you do not understand.

CULTURE NOTES
Looking for a Job

Looking for a job in North America can be different from looking for a job in your country. When you are getting ready for your job search, you need to understand how people look for a job in this country.

4   TEAM WORK

Work in small groups. Read the situations. Then discuss the questions. What does your group think? Write down your group's answers.

1. Thom is an actor. He came to the United States eight months ago. He can't find a job as an actor. He is looking for an entry-level job as a waiter now. Do you think that this is a good idea? Why or why not?

   _____

2. Kara needs to find a job. How many hours should she look for a job each week? Why?

   _____

3. Gabriel and Stewart applied for the same job as an office clerk. They both have good work skills. Gabriel has more experience, but Stewart was friendlier when he talked to the manager. Who do you think will get the job? Why?

   _____

4. Josie was a housewife in her country. She is looking for a job now. What skills does Josie have that will help her in a job? What skills can she talk about when she meets a manager?

   _____

5 TEAM WORK

Form new groups. Find classmates who were not in your group in
Exercise 4.

1. Compare your answers in Exercise 4. Which answers are the same?
    Which answers are different?

2. Now talk about *your* country. Discuss the questions in Exercise 4 again.

6 APPLY YOURSELF

Outside of class, ask two people who are working now these questions.
What do they say? Write down their answers.

1. Thom is an actor. He came to the United States eight months ago. He
    can't find a job as an actor. He is looking for an entry-level job as a
    waiter now. Do you think that this is a good idea? Why or why not?

    Person #1: _____

    Person #2: _____

2. Kara needs to find a job. How many hours should she look for a job
    each week? Why?

    Person #1: _____

    Person #2: _____

3. Gabriel and Stewart applied for the same job as an office clerk. They
    both have good work skills. Gabriel has more experience, but Stewart
    was friendlier when he talked to the manager. Who do you think will
    get the job? Why?

    Person #1: _____

    Person #2: _____

4. Josie was a housewife in her country. She is looking for a job now.
    What skills does Josie have that will help her in a job? What skills can
    she talk about when she meets a manager?

    Person #1: _____

    Person #2: _____

7 TEAM WORK

Work in small groups. Discuss your answers in Exercise 6.

Personal Qualities

When you are looking for a job, you need to think about your personal qualities. What kind of person are you? What makes you a good worker? It is important to know your qualities because this will help you to choose your short-term and long-term goals.

You also need to know your personal qualities because you need to tell managers about yourself. You need to tell managers that you are a good person for the job you want. When you tell managers about your personal qualities, you need to give examples from your past job (or jobs) or from your life.

8 LISTENING

You will hear eight people talking about their personal qualities. Which two personal qualities does each person talk about? Circle the correct letters.

1. a. I'm patient.
   b. I'm energetic.
   c. I'm organized.
   d. I'm good with numbers.

2. a. I work well with people.
   b. I'm efficient.
   c. I work well under pressure.
   d. I'm patient.

3. a. I'm reliable.
   b. I'm a fast learner.
   c. I'm organized.
   d. I'm flexible.

4. a. I'm creative.
   b. I'm a hard worker.
   c. I'm a fast learner.
   d. I'm strong.

5. a. I'm efficient.
   b. I work well under pressure.
   c. I'm energetic.
   d. I work well with people.

6. a. I'm creative.
   b. I'm flexible.
   c. I'm careful with details.
   d. I'm a fast learner.

7. a. I'm a good problem solver.
   b. I'm careful with details.
   c. I'm good with my hands.
   d. I'm good with numbers.

8. a. I'm a good problem solver.
   b. I'm good with numbers.
   c. I'm reliable.
   d. I'm energetic.

9 WORDS FOR SUCCESS

Read the personal qualities in the left column. Read the examples of these qualities in the right column. Match each personal quality with the correct example. Write *a* or *b* on each line.

b 1. I am *careful with details*.

    2. I am *efficient*.

a. I work very fast, and my work is excellent.

b. My work is always correct because I check it carefully.

___ 3. I am *strong*.

a. I'm relaxed when work is slow or boring. I can do routine work.

___ 4. I am *patient*.

b. I can lift heavy boxes. I always help my friends when they move to new apartments.

___ 5. I am *reliable*.

a. I like to work as part of a team, and I like to help people. I'm friendly.

___ 6. I *work well with people*.

b. I always come to work on time, and I always finish my work. When I say I will do something, I always do it.

___ 7. I am *good with my hands*.

a. When my work is difficult or I am very busy, I am relaxed. I always meet my deadlines (finish my work on time).

___ 8. I *work well under pressure*.

b. I often build furniture for my family and friends.

___ 9. I am *organized*.

a. I make household schedules and plans. I can easily find the things I need.

___ 10. I am *flexible*.

b. I'm happy when my duties change at work. I can do many jobs at the same time.

___ 11. I am *a good problem solver*.

a. I don't take long breaks. If I don't finish my work, I work overtime.

___ 12. I am *a hard worker*.

b. When my supervisor gives me difficult work, I can find the answers easily.

___ 13. I am *good with numbers*.

a. I do math quickly, and I organize my household money well.

___ 14. I am *energetic*.

b. I have a lot of energy. I like to be busy.

___ 15. I am *creative*.

a. When my supervisor teaches me something new, I understand and learn quickly.

___ 16. I am *a fast learner*.

b. I like to think of new ideas. I always think of new activities for my children when they are bored.

10 TEAM WORK

Work in small groups. Look at the personal qualities listed in the box. Then take turns reading the situations to your classmates. Write the correct personal quality after each situation.

PART A

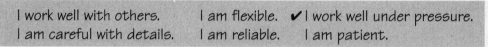

I work well with others.	I am flexible.	✔ I work well under pressure.
I am careful with details.	I am reliable.	I am patient.

1. "In my last job, I was a nurse's assistant. I worked in a hospital. When there was an emergency, I was very relaxed and careful."

   <u>I work well under pressure.</u>

2. "In my last job, I was an auto mechanic. When my boss asked me to fix cars, he didn't worry because he knew my work was very good. I never stayed home from work. I didn't go home before my work was finished because my customers needed their cars quickly."

   _____

3. "In my last job, I was a teacher's assistant, and I like to work with different kinds of people and talk about new ideas with them. I always helped my co-workers (the people I worked with) if they had problems or questions."

   _____

4. "When I work, I like to do a good job. At my last job, I was a bookeeping assistant. My work had to be neat and correct. After I finished my work, I always looked at my math again, so there were no mistakes."

   _____

5. "I like to do different things at work. In my last job, I was a cook in a restaurant. I cooked, answered the phone, and helped customers at the same time. When my co-workers were sick, I was happy to work for them."

   _____

6. "I worked in a lab. Sometimes my work was very interesting, but other times I needed to do the same thing again and again. The work wasn't always interesting, but I knew it was important. So I did it well."

   _____

PART B

I am organized.	I am a hard worker.	I am good with my hands.
I am a fast learner.	I am good with numbers.	I am efficient.

7. "I really like to work hard. In my last job, I was a baker's assistant in a busy bakery. When we were very busy, I stayed late to finish my work."

   _____

8. "In my last job, I worked in a bank. I took money from customers and gave money to them. I can count well, so my math was always correct."

   _____

9. "When I started my last job, I needed to learn so many new things. I listened carefully to my boss and co-workers. I watched them work, and I asked a lot of questions. In only two weeks, I understood how to do my job."

_____

10. "In my last job, I repaired watches. I worked with small parts, and I used many small tools. My watches always worked well."

_____

11. "In my last job, I was a file clerk. I made a list of what I needed to do every day. My files and desk were very neat, so I could always find the papers I needed."

_____

12. "In my last job, I was a cashier in a grocery store. I worked on the express line because I was very fast and I didn't make mistakes."

_____

11 ON YOUR OWN

Look at pages 6 and 7 again. Choose three of _your_ best personal qualities from the ones listed there. Write them down. Then give your own examples of each quality (like the stories in Exercise 10).

EXAMPLE:

PERSONAL QUALITY: _I'm flexible._

For example, _I was the manager of a clothing store. I did many different things at my job. I answered customers' questions, I ordered clothes, and I helped the salespeople when they were busy._

1. PERSONAL QUALITY: _____

For example, _____

_____

_____

2. PERSONAL QUALITY: _____

For example, _____

_____

_____

3. PERSONAL QUALITY: _____

For example, _____

_____

_____

12   PAIR WORK

Work with a partner. Talk about your personal qualities that you chose and wrote about in Exercise 11.

JOB DUTIES

When you are looking for a job, you need to think about your past job and about what you did in your past job (your **job duties**). You need to know your past job duties so you can talk about your skills. It is important to know your job duties and your skills because this will help you to choose your goals.

You also need to know your past job duties because you will need to tell managers about your past job or jobs. You need to give examples from your past job or jobs so managers will understand what you did.

If you had a job in the past, you have **work experience**. If you did not have a job, and you do not have work experience, you need to think about your **life experience**. Did you drive a car? Did you repair televisions? Did you make clothes? Did you cook? Did you take care of children?

☊ 13   LISTENING

You will hear three people talking about their jobs. What was each person's job? Circle the correct letter.

1. What did Pedro do?

   a. He was a driver.
   b. He was a sales clerk.
   c. He was a gardener.
   d. He was a musician.

2. What did Lee do?

   a. He was a photo lab assistant.
   b. He was a baker's assistant.
   c. He was a lab assistant.
   d. He was a teacher's assistant.

3. What did Jade do?

   a. She was a cashier.
   b. She was a musician.
   c. She was an office clerk.
   d. She was a driver.

🎧 14 LISTENING

You will hear Pedro, Lee, and Jade talking about their jobs again. What were their job duties? Circle the correct letter or letters.

1. What were Pedro's job duties?

   a. He planted grass and flowers.
   b. He counted change.
   c. He practiced music.
   d. He cared for plants and trees.

2. What were Lee's job duties?

   a. He used kitchen equipment.
   b. He did lab tests.
   c. He cleaned and organized lab equipment.
   d. He cleaned the kitchen.

3. What were Jade's job duties?

   a. She used a cash register.
   b. She delivered things.
   c. She entered information into a computer.
   d. She collected cash, checks, and charge payments.

15 WORDS FOR SUCCESS: Job Dictionary

Now you will make a dictionary of **job titles** (the names of jobs) and the **job duties** for each of them. You can use this dictionary to help you find your job goals and to talk about your job duties.

Look at the pictures of entry-level jobs on pages 12–15. A job title is near each picture. Then look at the lists of job duties.

Match the job duties with the job titles. Write the correct job title on each line.

1. _____
   Measure and mix ingredients
   Use kitchen equipment
   Prepare and cook food

2. _____
   Take customers' orders
   Serve food
   Answer customers' questions

3. _____
   Mix and cut dough
   Bake bread, cookies, and cakes
   Clean kitchen

4. _____
   Set and clean tables
   Help waitresses and waiters
   Carry dishes and coffee

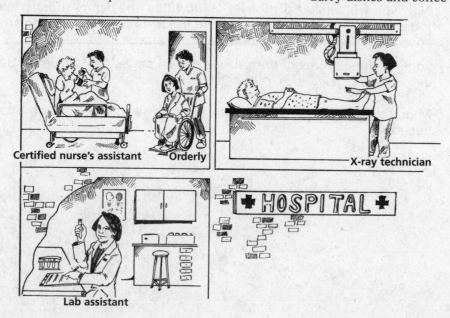

5. _____
   Move patients and equipment
   Clean hospital rooms and halls
   Feed and wash patients

6. _____
   Use X-ray equipment
   Give instructions to patients
   Move patients on table

7. _____
   Take temperature and blood pressure
   Answer patients' questions
   Help nurses and doctors

8. _____
   Clean and organize lab equipment
   Do lab tests
   Label test tubes

9. _____
   Install computer equipment
   Repair computer equipment
   Test computer equipment

10. _____
    Remove paint from walls
    Use brushes and ladders
    Paint houses, apartments, and offices

11. _____
    Enter information into a computer
    Sort mail
    Make photocopies

12. _____
    Watch people and grounds
    Check doors and windows
    Respond to emergencies

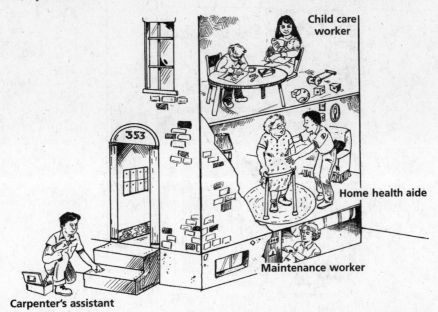

13. _____
    Care for elderly people
    Help disabled people
    Give medicine to sick people

14. _____
    Clean building and grounds
    Repair plumbing and wiring
    Respond to tenants' requests

15. _____
    Organize children's games, art, and activities
    Serve meals to children
    Help children eat and dress

16. _____
    Use hand and power tools
    Measure and cut wood
    Build stairs and cabinets

Salesclerk **Cashier** **Warehouse worker** **Driver**

17. _____
Move items by hand or with hand truck
Count and record items
Sort and put items on shelves

18. _____
Put items on shelves and tables
Answer customers' questions
Collect cash, checks, and charge payments

19. _____
Collect cash, checks, and charge payments
Use cash register
Count money and change

20. _____
Drive car or van
Deliver food, flowers, or other things
Collect money

Housekeeper **Health club attendant** **Musician** **Baggage porter** **Gardener**

21. _____
Read music
Practice music
Play music

22. _____
Carry hand baggage
Take guests to rooms
Move heavy items with handtrucks

23. _____
Clean rooms and halls
Make beds
Bring towels and soap to rooms

24. _____
Clean locker room and floors
Give and collect towels, keys, and equipment

Answer customers' questions

25. _____
Plant grass and flowers
Care for plants and trees
Use gardening tools and equipment

Teacher's assistant

Cosmetologist's assistant

Photo lab assistant

OUI'S GARAGE

Auto body repair person

Copy machine operator

26. _____
Remove parts
Repair parts
Paint repaired parts

27. _____
Wash hair
Polish nails
Clean the floor

28. _____
Help students with schoolwork
Organize classroom materials and equipment
Correct tests and homework

29. _____
Put paper in machines
Make photocopies
Collect money

30. _____
Read customer orders
Label order envelopes
Use photo printing machine

LANGUAGE FOCUS
Talking about Past Job Duties

When you talk about past job duties, use the past tense.

- With regular verbs, add *-ed* or *-d*:
  answer—answer*ed*
  use—use*d*

- With irregular verbs, you need to use a special form:
  bring—brought
  drive—drove
  feed—fed
  give—gave
  make—made
  put—put
  take—took
  set—set

16 PAIR WORK

Look again at the job titles and job duties on pages 12 to 15. What did each person do in his or her past job? Take turns answering the questions.

1. In his past job, Eddie was a painter. What did he do?

   He removed paint from walls. He used brushes and ladders. He painted houses, apartments, and offices.

2. In her past job, Anna was a cosmetology assistant. What did she do?

3. In his past job, Tariq was a cashier. What did he do?

4. In her past job, Kin was a general office clerk. What did she do?

5. In his past job, Bing was a driver. What did he do?

6. In her past job, Maria was a waitress. What did she do?

17 ON YOUR OWN

Write about your work experience. Use the dictionary on pages 12–15 to help you find your past job title and duties. If you cannot find your past job title and duties in the dictionary, ask someone who speaks your native language to help you.

If you did not have a job, then write about your life experience. What did you do every day? For example, Benita did not have a job, but she worked at home every day. She took care of her children. She cleaned her house and cooked. This is Benita's life experience.

Your past job title: _____

Your work experience or your life experience: _____

_____

_____

_____

WORK SKILLS AND LIFE SKILLS

When you are looking for a job, you need to think about your skills. What can you do? Your skills can be **work skills** (from your past job or jobs) or **life skills** (from your life).

To find your work skills, think about your past job duties. What did you do in your past job? What did you learn in your past job? For example, Alex was a nurse. He helped sick people. He gave them medicine.

Your work skills are what you can do now or in the future. For example, Alex can help sick people, and he can give them medicine. He can use these skills in his future job, too.

Maybe you are looking for a job now, but you didn't have a job in the past. Maybe your work skills from your past job won't help you in your future job. Then you need to think about your life skills.

To find your life skills, think about what you can do in your everyday life. For example: Can you drive a car? Can you repair televisions? Can you make clothes? Can you cook? Can you take care of children?

LANGUAGE FOCUS
Talking about Skills

When you talk about past job duties, you use the past tense. When you talk about skills, you use *can* or *know how to* and the simple form of the verb.

JOB DUTIES	WORK SKILLS
Eddie removed paint from walls.	He *can remove* paint from walls.
He used brushes and ladders.	He *knows how to use* brushes and ladders.
He painted houses and offices.	He *can paint* houses and offices.

LIFE SKILLS

Ella *knows how to drive* a car.

Sam *can repair* televisions.

18 PAIR WORK

Work with a partner. Read about five people's job duties. What are each person's skills? Take turns answering the questions. Use *can* and *know how to* and the simple form of the verb.

1. Anna was a cosmetology assistant. She washed hair, polished nails, and cleaned the floor. What are Anna's work skills?

   She can wash hair. She knows how to polish nails.
   She can clean the floor.

2. Tariq was a cashier. He collected cash, checks, and charge payments. He used a cash register. He counted money and change. What are Tariq's work skills?

3. Kin was a general office clerk. She entered information into a computer. She sorted mail. She made photocopies. What are Kin's work skills?

4. Bing was a driver. He drove a car. He delivered things. He collected money. What are Bing's work skills?

5. Maria was a waitress. She took customers' orders. She served food. She answered customers' questions. What are Maria's work skills?

19 TEAM WORK

Work in small groups. Tell your classmates about your life skills. Make a list of everyone's life skills.

_____

_____

_____

_____

_____

20 TEAM REPORTS

Now tell your teacher and your other classmates about your group's life skills. How many life skills does your class have? Make a list with your teacher.

21 ON YOUR OWN

In Exercise 17, you wrote about your work experience or your life experience. Now write about your work skills and your life skills. Remember to use _can_ or _know how to_ and the simple form of the verb.

_____

_____

_____

_____

_____

TRANSFERABLE SKILLS

When you know your personal qualities and skills, you can find your job goal. You can find the best job for you, and you can decide what jobs are not good for you. When you apply for a job, you need to tell the manager about your personal qualities and skills that will best help you in the job you want. These are your **transferable skills.**

PERSONAL QUALITIES

What kind of work do you like to do? What kind of person are you? Think about your personal qualities. For example, Alex likes to work with people. There are many jobs where he can work with people. Sales clerks, waiters, and teacher's assistants all work with people.

WORK SKILLS AND LIFE SKILLS

What kind of work can you do? Think about your work skills and your life skills. For example, Alex can help sick people, so maybe he will look for a job as a home health aide or for a job in a hospital.

 BE CAREFUL: Do *not* tell the manager about personal qualities and skills that will *not* help you in the job you want. For example, if you are applying for a job as a home health aide, do *not* say that you know how to repair cars.

⌖ 22 LISTENING

Yolanda and her friend, Aree, are talking about Yolanda's goals. Read the questions. Then listen to the conversation. Circle the correct letter or letters.

1. What was Yolanda's last job?

   a. She was a waitress.
   b. She was an office clerk.
   c. She was a teacher.
   d. She was a technician.

2. Why does Yolanda need to choose a short-term job goal?

   a. She didn't like her last job.
   b. She wants to study.
   c. She doesn't have work experience.
   d. She doesn't have a certificate.

3. What personal qualities do Yolanda and Aree talk about?

   a. She is energetic.
   b. She is patient.
   c. She is organized.
   d. She is creative.

4. Aree talks about a short-term job goal for Yolanda. What is it?

   a. She can be a waitress.
   b. She can be an office clerk.
   c. She can be a teacher.
   d. She can be a technician.

5. What work skills do Yolanda and Aree talk about?

   a. She can correct tests.
   b. She can teach classes.
   c. She can answer questions from students and parents.
   d. She can talk to students and help them with their schoolwork.

6. What life skills do Yolanda and Aree talk about?

   a. She's good with her hands.
   b. She's good with children.
   c. She can repair cars.
   d. She's good with numbers.

⌕ 23 LISTENING

Listen again to the conversations in Exercise 22. Then discuss these questions with your classmates.

1. Which of Yolanda's *personal qualities* are transferable to a job as a waitress? Why?

2. Which of Yolanda's *work skills* are transferable to a job as a waitress? Why?

3. Which of Yolanda's *life skills* are transferable to a job as a waitress? Why?

24 ON YOUR OWN

Read about some people who are looking for jobs. Which jobs are good for each person? Which jobs are not good? Think about each person's transferable skills (personal qualities, work skills, and life skills). You can look at pages 12–15 to read the duties for the possible jobs.

Number the jobs like this:

1 = the best job
2 = a very good job
3 = a good job
4 = not a good job

There may be more than one correct way to number the jobs.

1. Jana was a sales clerk. She likes to work with people. She also likes to cut her friends' hair.

___ cook

___ cashier

___ computer technician

___ cosmetology assistant

2. Sergei was an electronics technician. He knows how to repair televisions and can use tools. His workplace is always very clean and organized.

___ carpenter's assistant

___ stock clerk

___ hotel housekeeper

___ maintenance worker

3. Angela stayed at home and took care of her house and children. She is patient, and she is very good at fixing things.

___ automobile body repair person

___ home health aide

___ baker's assistant

___ child care worker

4. Eleni was a factory worker. She is efficient, and she is very careful with details.

___ waitress

___ security guard

___ laboratory assistant

___ general office clerk

25 TEAM WORK

Work in small groups. Compare your answers in Exercise 24. Do you agree or disagree with each other? Why? Talk about the transferable skills in each situation.

26 ON YOUR OWN

Now think about what jobs are best for you:

What kind of person are you? Look at your personal qualities on page 9.
What kind of work can you do? Look at your skills on page 19.
What kind of work do you like to do? What jobs are best for you? Look at the dictionary of jobs and job duties on pages 12–15, and think about other jobs that you know about.

Write down your job goals.

What is your short-term goal? _____

What is your long-term goal? _____

27 TEAM WORK

Work in small groups. Take turns telling your classmates your *short-term* job goal. Then talk about your skills and personal qualities. Which skills and personal qualities will help you in the job you want? What are your transferable skills for your short-term job goal?

28 ON YOUR OWN

Write your transferable skills for your *short-term* job goal:

EXAMPLE:

SHORT-TERM JOB GOAL: Driver

Transferable Skills

    Personal qualities: work well with people
        good with details

    Work skills and life skills: can read maps
        can drive car or van
        can collect money

YOUR SHORT-TERM JOB GOAL:

Transferable Skills

Your personal qualities:

Your work skills and life skills:

YOUR JOB SEARCH

When you know your short-term job goal and your transferable skills, you are ready to look for a job. First you need to find **job openings**. Where are the jobs? Which companies need workers?

After you find job openings, you need to **contact** (call or write) businesses so managers know that you are interested in a job.

When managers are interested in you, they will want to meet you.

HOW TO FIND A JOB

Here are three ways to find job openings:

- **Walk in:** Go into businesses and ask about jobs. Sometimes you will see "Help Wanted" signs.
- **Network:** Talk to family, friends, and other people you know. Tell them you are looking for a job.
- **Use the want ads:** Many businesses put information about jobs in the newspaper. Look in the newspaper and read about job openings.

Here are three ways to contact businesses:

- **Make telephone calls** to businesses: Talk to managers and introduce yourself.
- **Fill out job applications:** Write information about yourself and your past jobs on company forms.
- **Send your resume:** Mail typed information about your skills, your past jobs, and your education.

After you contact businesses, you need to:

- **Go to interviews:** Managers who are interested in you want to meet you face-to-face and find out about your experience, your skills, and your personal qualities. Managers do not usually give you a job before they meet you.

☊ 29 LISTENING

Alex and May are talking about their new jobs. Read the questions. Then listen to the conversation. Circle the correct letter or letters.

1. What is Alex's new job?

   a. carpenter
   b. busperson
   c. hospital orderly
   d. baggage porter

2. How did Alex find his new job?

   a. He read the want ads.
   b. He sent his resume.
   c. He walked in.
   d. He networked.

3. What did Alex do after he found out about the job?

   a. He called the manager.
   b. He filled out an application.
   c. He sent his resume.
   d. He had an interview.

4. What is May's new job?

   a. nurse's assistant
   b. photo lab assistant
   c. baker's assistant
   d. carpenter's assistant

5. How did May look for job openings?

   a. She read the want ads.
   b. She filled out job applications.
   c. She walked in.
   d. She networked.

6. What did May do after she found out about some jobs?

   a. She sent her resume.
   b. She filled out an application.
   c. She called the manager.
   d. She had an interview.

HOW YOU CAN FIND A JOB

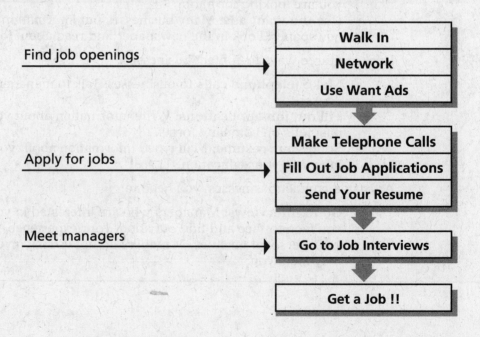

30 PAIR WORK

INFORMATION GAP: Student A, look at this page. Student B, look at page 210.

You and your partner will read a story about Yolanda's job search. This story has two parts.

1.   Read Part A of the story to yourself.

2.   Then tell your story to your partner in your own words.

3.   Ask your partner the questions following your story.

4.   Listen to your partner tell you Part B of the story and answer his or her questions.

PART A: YOLANDA'S JOB SEARCH

Yolanda Romero was a teacher in Mexico. She moved to Los Angeles three years ago. She wanted to be a teacher in the United States, but she needed to study English. She also needed a teaching certificate.

Yolanda wanted to work with people, so she decided to be a waitress. She looked for "Help Wanted" signs in restaurants and read the want ads in the newspaper every Sunday. Then she called about the job openings.

Yolanda looked for a job for three months. She worried about her future, but her friends said, "Don't worry. Sometimes it takes a long time to find a job in the United States."

One day Yolanda saw a "Help Wanted" sign in a restaurant. She walked in and talked to the manager. She filled out an application. The manager called her the next week, and she got a job as a waitress. She was very happy to get her first job in the United States.

1.   What did Yolanda do in Mexico?

2.   What was Yolanda's long-term goal when she came to the United States? Why couldn't she get that job?

3.   What was Yolanda's short-term goal in the United States?

4.   What did Yolanda do when she was looking for her first job in the United States?

5.   How long did it take Yolanda to find her first job?

6.   How did Yolanda find her first job?

7.   What was Yolanda's first job?

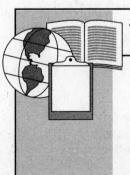

WHAT DO YOU THINK NOW?

Discuss these questions with your classmates.

1.   What do you need to think about and prepare before you look for a job?

2.   Why is it a good idea to take an entry-level job if you cannot find the job you want?

3.   How can you find job openings in this country?
     What do you need to do after you find job openings?

31 REVIEW: Name Game

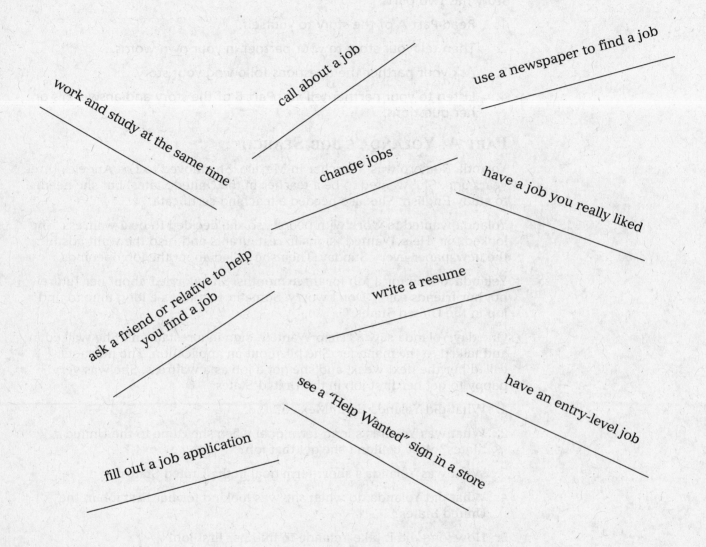

work and study at the same time

call about a job

use a newspaper to find a job

change jobs

have a job you really liked

ask a friend or relative to help
you find a job

write a resume

see a "Help Wanted" sign in a store

have an entry-level job

fill out a job application

Work with your classmates. Ask and answer questions about past jobs
and looking for a job. Use the phrases above with "Did you ever. . . ?"

Question: Did you ever *work and study at the same time*?

Answer: Yes, I did. / No, I didn't.

If your classmate says "Yes," write his or her name on the line, and then
ask another classmate a different question. If your classmate says "No,"
ask him or her another question or ask another classmate the same
question. Write a different name on each line.

Starting Your Job Search

WHAT DO YOU THINK?

Discuss these questions with your classmates.

1. When you walk into a company to ask about job openings, what should you say to the receptionist?
   What should you say to the manager?

2. What job information can you find out from a want ad?

3. Do people network in your country?
   Who do people network with in your country?
   Who can you network with in this country?

In this unit, you will:

- Learn about three good ways to look for a job:
  - Walking into companies
  - Looking at want ads
  - Networking
- Learn what you need to say when you ask for a job application.
- Learn how to read want ads in the newspaper.
- Learn how to ask people you know to help you find a job.

WALKING IN: TALKING TO A RECEPTIONIST OR ANOTHER EMPLOYEE

Stores, restaurants, hotels, and offices sometimes put "Help Wanted" signs in the window when they have job openings. When a business has a job opening, this business is looking for a new worker. When you see "Help Wanted" signs, you can go into companies and ask about jobs. This is called "walking in." Sometimes companies have job openings, but they don't put up signs. You can also walk into these companies and ask about jobs. When you walk into a company, the first person you talk to is usually the receptionist or another employee. Later, you can sometimes talk to the manager.

🎧 1 LISTENING

Alicia Sanchez is looking for a job. Read the questions. Then listen to the conversation. Circle the correct letter or letters.

1. Where is Alicia Sanchez?

    a. in a hospital
    b. in a hotel
    c. in a restaurant

2. Who is she talking to?

    a. the manager
    b. a friend
    c. an employee

3. What job is she looking for?

    a. a job as a housekeeper
    b. a job as a hospital orderly
    c. a job as a cook

4. What does Alicia ask for?

    a. an application
    b. the manager's name
    c. the working hours

5. When will the manager come back?

    a. this afternoon
    b. next week
    c. tomorrow morning

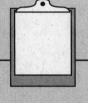

HOW TO TALK TO A RECEPTIONIST OR ANOTHER EMPLOYEE

When you talk to the receptionist or another employee, you need to do these things:

- Introduce yourself.
- Say that you are looking for a job.
- Ask to speak to the manager.

When the manager is *not* in, you also need to do these things:

- Ask for an application.
- Ask for the manager's name.
- Ask when the manager will be in.
- Say "thank you."

---

2 WORDS FOR SUCCESS

Match the sentences on the left with the sentences on the right. Write the correct number on each line. Each number can be used more than once.

WHAT TO DO

1. Introduce yourself.

2. Say that you are looking for a job.

3. Ask to speak to the manager.

WHAT TO SAY

___ May I speak to the person who does the hiring, please?

_1_ My name is . . .

___ I'm . . .

___ Could I talk to the manager, please?

___ I'm interested in a job . . .

___ I'm looking for a job . . .

When the Manager Isn't There

4. Ask for an application.

5. Ask for the manager's name.

6. Ask when the manager will be in.

7. Say "thank you."

___ Could you tell me the manager's name, please?

___ Thank you for your help.

_4_ Could I fill out an application, please?

___ Could you tell me when the manager will be available, please?

___ May I have the manager's name, please?

___ Thank you very much.

___ May I have an application, please?

___ Could you tell me when the manager will be in, please?

⌒ 3 LISTENING

You will hear three people asking about jobs. What does each person say? Check (✔) the correct column.

	1	2	3
My name is . . .			
I'm . . .			
I'm interested in a job . . .			
I'm looking for a job . . .			
Could I talk to the manager, please?			
May I speak to the person who does the hiring, please?			
May I have an application, please?			
Could I fill out an application anyway, please?			
Could you tell me the manager's name, please?			
May I have the manager's name, please?			
Could you tell me when the manager will be in, please?			
Could you tell me when the manager will be available, please?			
Thank you very much.			
Thank you for your help.			

 4 LISTENING

Listen again to the conversations in Exercise 3. Then discuss these questions with your classmates.

1. In which conversations did the applicant forget something?
2. What did he or she forget?

LANGUAGE FOCUS
Polite Requests

When you ask someone to help you, it is important to use polite language. Compare the sentences on the left with the requests on the right. Which are more polite?

I want to go home early.	*Could I* go home early, *please*?
Give me a pen.	*May I* have a pen, *please*?
What's the manager's name?	*Could you* tell me the manager's name, *please*?

It is also possible to say *please* after *you* or *I*. For example, "Could you *please* tell me the manager's name?"

BE CAREFUL: You cannot say "May you . . ." in English.

---

5 PAIR WORK

Work with a partner. Change the sentences to polite requests with *Could I, Could you,* or *May I.* Don't forget to use *please.*

1. I want to talk to the manager.
2. What's the manager's last name?
3. Spell the manager's name.
4. When can I see the manager?
5. I want an application.

6 PAIR WORK

Complete the applicant's part of the conversations on this page and the next, using the sentences in the box. Then practice the conversations with a partner.

PART A

> Thank you. Could you tell me when the manager will be in, please?
> Could I talk to the manager, please?
> Yes. Could I fill out an application anyway, please?
> And could you tell me the manager's name, please?
> ✔ I'm looking for a job as a baggage porter.
> Vivian Turner. Thank you very much.

Receptionist: Good morning.

Applicant: Hello. My name is Jeff Kao.

I'm looking for a job as a baggage porter.

_____

Receptionist: I'm sorry. She isn't here right now, and we don't have any openings. Can I help you?

Applicant: _____

Receptionist: Certainly. Here you are.

Applicant: _____

Receptionist: She'll be in this afternoon.

Applicant: _____

Receptionist: Sure. Her name is Vivian Turner.

Applicant: _____

Receptionist: You're welcome.

PART B

> Could you tell me when the manager will be available, please?
> Walter Breen. Okay, I'll come back at 3:00. Thank you very much.
> Thank you. And may I have the manager's name, please?
> I saw your "Help Wanted" sign in the window, and I'm interested in a job.
> May I have an application anyway, please?

Employee: Good afternoon. May I help you?

Applicant: Good afternoon. I'm Jennifer Beach.

_____

May I speak to the person who does the hiring?

Employee: I'm afraid the manager isn't in right now.

Applicant: _____

Employee: Sure. Here you are.

Applicant: _____

Employee: He'll be in at 3:00 P.M. today.

Applicant: _____

Employee: Certainly. His name is Walter Breen.

Applicant: _____

Employee: You're welcome.

7 ROLE PLAYS

INFORMATION GAP: Student A, look at this page. Student B, look at page 211.

Work with a partner. Read the first situation. Then create a conversation. When you finish, read the second situation. Create another conversation.

1. You are looking for a job as (your job goal). You walk into a business and talk to the receptionist. Introduce yourself and say that you are looking for a job. If the manager isn't there, ask for an application, ask when the manager will be in, and ask for the manager's name.

2. You are a receptionist in a business. Student B is looking for a job. Your manager, Scott Lowe, is out now. He will be in tomorrow at 9:00 A.M.

Walking in: TALKING TO A MANAGER

After you talk to a receptionist or another employee, you can sometimes talk to the person who does the hiring. Sometimes this is a manager. Sometimes this is the **personnel director**, who can also be called the **human resources director**.

⌒ 8 LISTENING

Maw Win is looking for a job. Read the questions. Then listen to the conversation. Circle the correct letter or letters.

1. What job is Maw Win looking for?

   a. a job as a housekeeper
   b. a job as a cook
   c. a job as a cashier

2. Where is Maw Win?

   a. in a hospital
   b. in a hotel
   c. in a restaurant

3. What does Maw Win talk about?

   a. her experience
   b. her family
   c. her personal qualities

4. What information does Maw Win ask for?

   a. the salary
   b. when the job starts
   c. the hours of the job
   d. whether the job is full-time or part-time

HOW TO TALK TO A MANAGER

When you talk to the manager, you need to repeat some things that you said to the receptionist. You need to do these things:

- Introduce yourself.
- Say that you are looking for a job.
- Tell the manager about your experience or personal qualities.

When there are job openings, you need to do these things:

- Ask for an application or ask to leave a resume.
- Ask about the schedule (the days and hours of the job).
- Ask when the job begins.

When there are *no* job openings, you need to do these things:

- Ask for an application, or ask to leave a resume anyway.
- Ask if there will be job openings in the future.

9 WORDS FOR SUCCESS

Match the sentences on the left with the sentences on the right. Write the correct number on each line. Each number can be used more than once.

WHAT TO DO

1. Tell the manager about your personal qualities/skills.

2. Tell the manager about your experience.

If There Are Job Openings:

3. Ask to fill out an application.

4. Ask to leave a resume.

5. Ask about the hours of the job.

6. Ask when the job begins.

If There Are No Job Openings:

7. Ask to fill out a job application anyway.

8. Ask to leave a resume anyway.

9. Ask if there will be job openings in the future.

WHAT TO SAY

_1_ I'm reliable.

___ I worked at a restaurant for two years.

___ I have two years' experience.

___ I can cook very well.

___ Could you tell me the schedule, please?

___ May I leave a resume, please?

___ Could you tell me the starting date, please?

_3_ May I have an application, please?

___ Could you tell me the working hours, please?

___ Could you tell me when the job starts, please?

___ Could I give you my resume, please?

___ Could I fill out an application, please?

___ Could I give you my resume anyway, please?

___ Will there be any work here later on?

_7_ Could I fill out an application anyway, please?

___ May I leave a resume anyway, please?

___ Will you have any openings in the future?

___ May I have an application anyway, please?

∩ 10 LISTENING

You will hear three people asking about jobs. What does each person say? Check (✔) the correct column.

	1	2	3
I'm (personal quality).			
I know how to (work skill).			
I worked at (a workplace) for (months).			
I have _____ year's experience.			
Could I fill out an application, please?			
May I have an application anyway, please?			
Could you tell me the working hours, please?			
Could you tell me when the job starts, please?			
May I leave a resume, please?			
Could I leave my resume anyway, please?			
Will you have any openings in the future?			
Will there be any work here later on?			

∩ 11 LISTENING

Listen again to the conversations in Exercise 10. Then discuss these questions with your classmates.

1. In which conversation is there a job opening?

2. In which conversation did the applicant forget something? What did he or she forget?

12 PAIR WORK

Work with a partner. Change the sentences to polite requests with *Could I, Could you,* or *May I.* Don't forget to use *please.*

1. Tell me when the job starts.

2. Tell me the hours.

3. I want to fill out an application anyway.

4. I want to leave a resume.

5. Give me your business card.

6. Give me your phone number.

CULTURE NOTES

Body Language and Personal Appearance

When you meet a manager, your English language is important, but your body language is important, too. For example, if you smile, the manager will think you are friendly. If you make eye contact (look at the manager's face) and stand straight, the manager will think that you are confident.

Your personal appearance also says something about you. For example, your hair should look nice, and your clothes should be neat and professional. If you are careful with your personal appearance, the manager will think that you will be careful with your job, too.

You can wear different kinds of clothes for different jobs. It is a good idea to find out what people usually wear for the job you are applying for. When you meet a manager, always wear clothes that are a little nicer than the clothes people usually wear for that job. Women usually wear a dress, a skirt and a blouse, or a suit. Men usually wear a jacket, tie, and nice pants, or a suit.

Here are some things to remember when you meet a manager:

- Look professional. Wear conservative clothes, jewelry, and makeup.
- Smile and make eye contact.
- Give a firm handshake (not too soft, not too hard).
- Stand two to three feet away from the manager.
- Speak clearly.
- Be enthusiastic.

"You never get a second chance to make a first impression."

13 TEAM WORK

Work in small groups. Talk about the job applicants in the four pictures on the next page. Talk about their body language and their personal appearance.

1. What do you think about their clothes, jewelry, hair, makeup . . . ?

2. What are they doing with their eyes, hands, legs, head, shoulders . . . ?

3. Do they look enthusiastic and friendly? Why or why not?

4. Are they doing anything that is not polite?

5. Are they standing too close or too far away from the manager?

A.

B.

14 ON YOUR OWN

What should you do when you meet a manager? What shouldn't you do?
Write sentences, using the phrases in the box.

✔ stand two to three feet away from the manager	speak very softly
✔ wear a lot of perfume or aftershave	smoke
wear big jewelry	smile
wear conservative clothes	be enthusiastic
look down	use a soft handshake
make eye contact	stand straight

Dos

1. You should stand two to three feet away from the manager.

2. _____

3. _____

4. _____

5. _____

6. _____

Don'ts

1. You shouldn't wear a lot of perfume or aftershave.

2. _____

3. _____

4. _____

5. _____

6. _____

15 TEAM WORK

Work in small groups. Compare your answers in Exercise 14. Are they the
same or different? Can you think of any other things you should or
shouldn't do when you meet a manager?

16 PAIR WORK

Complete the applicant's part of the conversations on this page and the
next, using the sentences in the box. Then practice the conversations
with a partner.

PART A

> May I have an application, please?
> 5:00 P.M. to 12:00 A.M. sounds great! I want to work at night.
> Thank you very much.
> ✔ I worked as a driver for six months, and I'm very reliable.
> Could you tell me the working hours, please?
> Thank you. Could you tell me when the job starts?

Manager: Can I help you?

Applicant: Yes. My name is Ruth Lee, and I'm interested in a job as a driver.

    I worked as a driver for six months, and I'm very reliable.

Manager: That's good. We have an opening for a driver now.

Applicant: _____

Manager: Certainly. Here you are.

Applicant: _____

Manager: It starts next Monday.

Applicant: _____

Manager: 5:00 P.M. to 12:00 A.M.

Applicant: _____

Manager: Well, I'll look at your application and call you in a few days.

Applicant: _____

Manager: You're welcome.

PART B

Could I fill out an application, anyway?
Thanks a lot.
Okay. I'll call you in a few months.
I have two years' experience as a gardener, and I'm very creative.
Thank you. May I leave my resume, too?
Thanks. Will you have any openings in the future?

Manager:	May I help you?
Applicant:	Yes. I'm Paul Susantos, and I'm looking for a job as a gardener.
	_____
Manager:	I'm afraid we don't have any openings now.
Applicant:	_____
Manager:	Certainly. Here's an application.
Applicant:	_____
Manager:	Sure. This looks like a nice resume!
Applicant:	_____
Manager:	Well, maybe in a few months.
Applicant:	_____
Manager:	That sounds fine.
Applicant:	_____

17 ROLE PLAYS

INFORMATION GAP: Student A, look at this page. Student B, look at page 211.

Work with a partner. Read the first situation. Then create a conversation. When you finish, read the second situation. Create another conversation.

1. Student A, you are a job applicant. Student B is the manager of a business. You are looking for a job as (your job goal). You saw a "Help Wanted" sign in the window.

   Don't forget to:

   • Tell the manager about your skills, qualities, or experience.

   • Ask for an application or to leave a resume.

   • Ask when the job starts.

   • Ask about the schedule.

2. Student A, you are the manager of a business. Student B is a job applicant. You do not have any job openings in your business now, but maybe you will have an opening next month.

Want ads

HEADINGS

You can look for jobs in the newspaper. First you need to find the **classified ads**. When people talk about classified ads, they often say **want ads**. There are many different parts in the classified ads, called **headings**. You need to find the heading that is about jobs. Different newspapers have different headings for jobs in the classified ads. Sometimes you need to look under these headings: *Help Wanted, Job Opportunities*, or *Employment* to find jobs.

 BE CAREFUL: Many headings are *not* about jobs. For example, some headings are about renting an apartment: *Rentals*. Some headings are about things for sale: *Sales/Merchandise*.

 BE CAREFUL: Sometimes people who are looking for jobs advertise in the classified ads. These ads are listed under headings like *Jobs Wanted, Employment Wanted*, or *Positions Wanted*. You *cannot* find job openings under these headings.

18 PAIR WORK

Here are some classified ad headings. Under which heading can you look for jobs? Check (✔) the correct headings.

✔ EMPLOYMENT

___ REAL ESTATE

___ SERVICES

___ JOBS WANTED

___ JOB OPPORTUNITIES

___ HELP WANTED

___ POSITIONS WANTED

___ RENTALS

SUBHEADINGS

After you find the heading *Employment, Job Opportunities*, or *Help Wanted*, you will sometimes find other headings that can help you find one kind of job. These are called **subheadings.** For example, you can look under the subheading *Skilled Trades* if you have special skills. A driver, an auto body repair person, and a carpenter have special skills and can find a job under *Skilled Trades*.

You can sometimes find a job under two different subheadings. For example, if you are looking for a job as a driver, you should look under the subheadings *Skilled Trades* and *General/Miscellaneous*.

19 PAIR WORK

Work with a partner. Read the subheadings. Where can you find the following jobs?

child care worker
sales clerk
waiter/waitress
office worker
housekeeper
home health aide
painter
hospital orderly
security guard

DOMESTIC HELP/ CHILD CARE	SKILLED TRADES	RESTAURANT/ HOTEL	SALES/ RETAIL
GENERAL/ MISCELLANEOUS	OFFICE/ CLERICAL	MEDICAL/ HEALTH CARE	

20 TEAM WORK

Bring a local newspaper to class. Work in small groups. Where can you look for a job that you want? Write the headings and subheadings.

HEADINGS	SUBHEADINGS
_____	_____
_____	_____
_____	_____

HOW TO UNDERSTAND ABBREVIATIONS

Businesses usually use abbreviations in the want ads. Want ads cost less money when businesses use abbreviations. An abbreviation is a short way to write a word. These rules will help you read abbreviations in want ads. Sometimes people use different abbreviations. For example, experience = exp., expr., exper.

Here are some examples of abbreviations you can find in the want ads:

Rule 1: Some abbreviations are the first letters of words.

sal.	=	salary
co.	=	company

Rule 2: Sometimes people take out letters (especially vowels):

intvw.	=	interview
appt.	=	appointment

Rule 3: Some abbreviations are the first letter of each word. Sometimes these abbreviations have a slash (/).

m/f	=	male/female
FT	=	full time

21 ON YOUR OWN

Write the number of the correct word next to each abbreviation.

1. The office hours are 8 in the morning to 5 in the afternoon, Monday through Friday.

   (a) ofc. _1_ (b) P.M _4_ (c) A.M. _3_ (d) M–F _5_ (e) hrs _2_.

2. Driver, male or female, with a minimum of 2 years experience.

   (a) yrs. ____ (b) exp. ____ (c) min. ____ (d) w/ ____ (e) m/f ____

3. Good position in small business. Equal Opportunity Employer.

   (a) sm. ____ (b) EOE ____ (c) gd. ____ (d) pos. ____ (e) bus. ____

4. Great opportunity. For interview, call Peter Cole at (414) 372-9809, extension 356, between 10 and 2.

   (a) intrvw. ____ (b) ext. ____ (c) btwn. ____ (d) oppty. ____ (e) grt. ____

5. Full-time sales clerk. Experience or training necessary. Management background preferred.

   (a) pref. ____ (b) F/T ____ (c) nec. ____ (d) bkgrd. ____ (e) trng. ____

6. Assistant manager, restaurant. Motivated, organized, high school graduate, second language a plus.

   (a) organ. ____ (b) a + ____ (c) mgr. ____ (d) asst. ____ (e) H.S. grad. ____

7. Permanent, part-time position. Must work weekends. Begins immediately.

   (a) immed. ____ (b) P/T ____ (c) wknds. ____ (d) perm. ____ (e) beg. ____

8. Large business seeks flexible individual for stock clerk. Write Post Office Box #729, St. Louis, MO 63188.

   (a) sks. ____ (b) flex. ____ (c) lg. ____ (d) P.O. ____ (e) indiv. ____

9. Temporary positions available for qualified technicians, experienced only. Days and evenings. Hourly wage.

   (a) temp. ____ (b) exp'd. ____ (c) hrly. ____ (d) dys./eves. ____ (e) avail. ____

10. Busy office needs people with excellent communication skills. Salary from $18,000. Send resume to 8818 8th Street, Seattle, WA 98112.

    (a) excl. ____ (b) St. ____ (c) res. ____ (d) nds. ____ (e) 18K ____

22 PAIR WORK

Work with a partner. Read the want ads. Then rewrite (write again) each ad according to the directions.

1. Rewrite the ads, using abbreviations.

Temporary, part-time sales position, 20 hours a week, 1 year experience necessary. Call Kit, 648-1215.

Small office needs organized individual to work copy machines. Male/Female. Fax resume to (612) 896-9362.

2. Rewrite the ads, using complete words.

Perm. FT driver needed. Valid lic. and car req'd. For appt., call John (813) 111-7731, ext. 630 betw. 9 & 12.

Lg. school sks. teaching asst. M–F am's. Teaching cert. nec. 2nd language a +. $7/hr. Call Ms. Marcus for intrvw. (212) 248-4892.

23 ON YOUR OWN

Create your own "dream ad." Write a want ad for a job you would like to have. Use abbreviations.

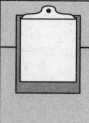

HOW TO APPLY FOR A JOB

A want ad gives a lot of information in a small space. When you find an ad for a job that you want, you need to read it carefully to find out how to apply for the job. There are three ways to apply for a job:

- Call the company and make an appointment.
- Go to the company and fill out an application.
- Send or fax a resume to the company.

24 ON YOUR OWN

Read the want ads. Find out how you should apply for each job. Write the information.

1. **Medical asst.** P/T evenings. Lic. required. X-ray exp. helpful but will train. Fax resume: 707-443-5626. Attn: Jana.

   Fax resume: 707-443-5626
   Attention: Jana

2. **Painter.** M/F. Need own car and tools. Temp. position. Call 914-0201. Ask for Ben.

3. **Security guard.** F/T. M–F, 8–5. M/F. Good pay. No exp. needed. Apply Tu–F, 9–12 at 43 Montgomery #600.

4. **Pharmacy clerk.** Mt. Herman Hosp. Exc. sal. 11pm–7am. 1 yr. exper. Send resume: TAD Resources, 1 Park Ave, Ste. 114, San Mateo, CA 94403.

5. **Retail sales.** F/T-P/T. Fashion Jewelry. Eves and wknds. Fax resume to Betsy. (617) 235-0137.

HOW TO UNDERSTAND INFORMATION ABOUT JOB REQUIREMENTS, QUALIFICATIONS, AND DUTIES

Here is some information you can find in want ads:

- The skills, experience, personal qualities, and other things you need to do the job
- Other skills or experience that employers want
- The work you will do at a job

You need to read a want ad very carefully to find out if you can do the job.

Requirements: Skills, experience, personal qualities, and other things you need for the job. For example, drivers need a driver's license and sometimes a car. Dental hygienists need a certificate. When you see *must, required* (req'd.), *necessary* (nec.), or *minimum* (min.), these are job requirements.

> FAMILY DAY CARE CENTER AIDE seeking **energetic, creative indiv.** for F/T pos. to help organize games, music and art. **Exper. nec. Must be 21 yrs. or older.** Bilingual preferred.

Preferred qualifications: Skills, experience, and other things that employers want. You do *not need* to have these, but they will help you get the job. When you see *preferred* (pref.), *helpful, desired,* or *a plus* (a +), these are preferred qualifications.

> FAMILY DAY CARE CENTER AIDE seeking energetic, creative indiv. for F/T pos. to help organize games, music and art. Exper. nec. Must be 21 yrs. or older. **Bilingual preferred.**

Job duties: The work you will do at a job. For example, apartment managers collect rent and fix things. When you see *responsible for* (respon. for), *to help,* or *duties include* (duties incl.), these are job duties.

> FAMILY DAY CARE CENTER AIDE seeking energetic, creative indiv. for F/T pos. **to help organize games, music and art.** Exper. nec. Must be 21 yrs. or older. Bilingual preferred.

25   PAIR WORK

Work with a partner. Read the want ads. Then fill in the chart.

		Job Duties	Job Requirements	Preferred Qualifications
1.	**Counterperson.** Must be friendly and reliable. Resp. for some baking and customer service. Second lang. a +.	Responsible for some baking and customer service	Must be friendly and reliable	Second language a plus
2.	**Office clerk** — to help with mail and typing. PC skills desired. Must be careful w/ details and a fast learner.			
3.	**Parking attendant.** Duties incl. parking cars and collecting fees. Gd. driving record nec. Exper. pref'd. but will train.			
4.	**Custodian/Janitor.** Resp. for clean-up and warehouse maintenance. Early AMs req'd. Own tools helpful.			
5.	**Bookkeeping assistant** — Duties incl. filing and assisting bookkeeper. Tax knowledge helpful. Min. 1 yr. exper.			

HOW TO UNDERSTAND OTHER INFORMATION ABOUT THE JOB

In many want ads, you can learn other information about the job. Sometimes you can find out this information:

- The hours
- The salary
- If the job is part-time or full-time
- If the job is temporary (for a short time) or permanent (for a long time)

26 PAIR WORK

Work with a partner. Read the want ads. Then fill in the chart.

CHILD CARE/ HOUSEKEEPER Enthusiastic person to care for 2 chldrn. Includes housekeeping. Must have own car. Nonsmoker only. Bilingual a+. Excl. sal. Call 326-8238.

COPY OPERATOR/ COUNTER SALES. Eve. shift. 4:30–12. Busy copy center nds. organized, energetic person to work copy machines and counter. 1+ yrs exp. pref. Apply in person at 4540 3rd St, NE, Washington, DC.

COMPUTER TECHNICIAN. Day shift in PC service co. Respon. for computer repair. Gd. pay. F/T perm pos. 2 yrs exp. req'd. Must know IBM computers. Fax res to Service Mgr (414) 264-9833.

Job Title	Child care/ Housekeeper		
How to Apply			
Job Requirements			
Preferred Qualifications		1+ year's experience	
Job Duties			
Other Information about the Job			Day shift in PC company Good pay Full-time Permanent

27 APPLY YOURSELF

Look at a local newspaper. Find want ads for three jobs that interest you. Put the ads in the boxes at the top (Want ad #1, Want ad #2, Want ad #3). Then fill in the chart.

Want ad #1   Want ad #2   Want ad #3

Job Title			
How to Apply			
Job Requirements			
Preferred Qualifications			
Job Duties			
Other Information about the Job			

28 TEAM WORK

Work in small groups. Tell your classmates about the three jobs you found in the newspaper.

JOB ANNOUNCEMENTS

Job announcements, also called **job listings**, have the same information as want ads, but you do *not* find job announcements in the newspaper. You can find job announcements at employment agencies (government or private offices that help people look for jobs). You can look in your local telephone book to find employment agencies in your city.

29 ON YOUR OWN

Read the job announcement. Then write the correct information about the job on the lines below.

MONARCH
JOB POSTING: POSITION AVAILABLE

Title _Warehouse Person_   Dept. _Warehouse_

Date Needed _Immediately_   Hours _11:00 A.M.–8:00 P.M._

Brief description of duties and responsibilities:

- Picking and restocking of products.
- Providing support in all areas of the warehouse.

Special knowledge, skill, and ability requirements:

- Must be able to lift 60 lbs. and more.
- Prefer someone with warehouse experience.

Education required:

- Requires a high school diploma.

If you are interested, please send your resume to the Human Resources Department.

133 Rose, Suite 115
San Francisco, CA 94108

Job title: _Warehouse Person_ _____

How to apply: _____

Job requirements: _____

Preferred qualifications: _____

Job duties: _____

Other information: _____

NETWORKING

Family, friends, neighbors, people you worked with in your last job, and other people you know can help you find a job. You need to tell these people that you are looking for a job. Ask them to help you. This is called **networking.** You can also network with social workers and job counselors. Sometimes people in your network know about jobs for you. Sometimes they don't know about any jobs, but they can ask their friends and other people. Many people in North America think that networking is the best way to find a job.

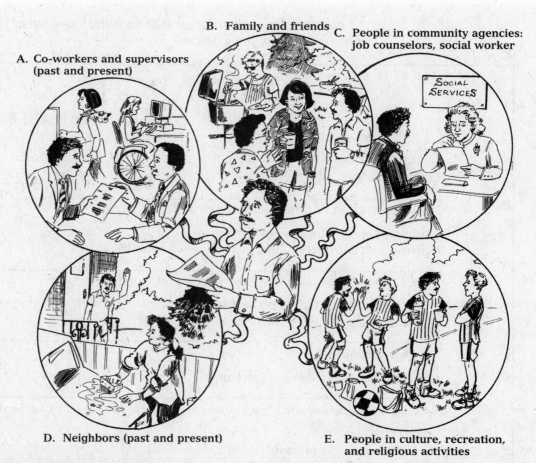

A. Co-workers and supervisors (past and present)

B. Family and friends

C. People in community agencies: job counselors, social worker

D. Neighbors (past and present)

E. People in culture, recreation, and religious activities

🎧 30   LISTENING

You will hear Kareem Halaj networking. Who is Kareem networking with in each conversation? Look at the pictures above. Write the correct letter next to each conversation.

___ Conversation # 1

___ Conversation # 2

___ Conversation # 3

___ Conversation # 4

___ Conversation # 5

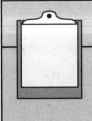

HOW TO NETWORK

When you network with someone, you need to do these things:

- Say hello.
- Say that you are looking for a job.
- Ask for help.
- Ask where you can look or who you can talk to.
- Ask the person to call you if he or she finds out about a job.
- Ask if you can give the person a resume.
- Say thank you.

31 WORDS FOR SUCCESS

Match the sentences on the left with the sentences on the right.
Write the correct number on each line. Each number can be used
more than once.

WHAT TO DO

1. Say hello.

2. Say that you are looking for a job.

3. Ask for help.

4. Ask where you can look or who you can talk to.

5. Ask the person to call you if he or she finds out about a job.

6. Ask if you can give the person a resume.

WHAT TO SAY

___ Could you help me?

___ May I send my resume to you?

_1_ Hi. How have you been?

___ I was wondering if you could help me.

___ Do you know anyone I could talk to?

___ If you find out about any jobs, could you call me?

___ I'm looking for a job . . .

___ Could I give you my resume?

___ If you hear of any jobs, could you call me?

___ Do you know where I could look?

___ I'm interested in working . . .

___ Hello. How are you?

⌒ 32 LISTENING

Listen again to the conversations in Exercise 30. What does Kareem say in each conversation? Check (✔) the correct column.

	1	2	3
How are you?			
How have you been?			
. . . I'm looking for a job.			
I'm interested in working . . .			
Could you help me?			
. . . I was wondering if you could help me.			
Do you know where I could look?			
Do you know anyone I could talk to?			
If you hear of any jobs, could you call me?			
If you find out about any jobs, could you call me?			
May I send you my resume?			
Could I give you my resume?			
Thanks a lot.			
Thank you very much . . .			

33 PAIR WORK

Jesse is looking for a job. He is networking with his friend, Maraya.
Complete Jesse's part of the conversation, using the sentences in the box.
Then practice the conversation with a partner.

> Great! Could I give you my resume, too?
> A job as a driver. Could you help me?
> ✔ Okay, I guess. But I'm looking for a job.
> Thanks. And do you know anyone I could talk to?
> Thanks a lot. I'll call you next week.
> If you hear of any jobs, could you call me?

Jesse: Hi, Maraya. How are you doing?

Maraya: Fine. And you?

Jesse: Okay, I guess. But I'm looking for a job.

Maraya: Really? What kind of job are you looking for?

Jesse: _____

Maraya: Maybe. What can I do?

Jesse: _____

Maraya: Sure. I'd be happy to call if I hear about any jobs.

Jesse: _____

Maraya: Well, maybe you could talk to my friend, Erica. She works in a
          big office supply company. I'll talk to her.

Jesse: _____

Maraya: That would be helpful. I'll give it to Erica when I see her.

Jesse: _____

Maraya: Okay. Goodbye.

34 ROLE PLAYS

INFORMATION GAP: Student A, look at this page. Student B, look at page 212.

Work with a partner. Read the first situation. Then create a conversation. When you finish, read the second situation. Create another conversation.

1. Student A, you are looking for a job as (your job goal). You are networking with Student B. Student B is your friend. Ask your friend to help you.

2. Student A, you are Student B's neighbor. Student B is looking for a job and asks you for help. Your friend, (name) , might know about a job opening. Tell Student B to call your friend. Tell Student B that your friend's telephone number is _____ .

Networking: FOLLOW-UP

After you network with someone, you usually need to take the next step. For example, sometimes you need to call someone. Sometimes you need to send someone your resume. This is called **follow-up**.

HOW TO FOLLOW UP AFTER YOU NETWORK

When you call someone to follow up after networking, you need to do these things:

- Say your name.
- Say the name of the person you networked with and your relationship to that person.
- Say that you are looking for a job.
- Ask about job openings.
- Say thank you.

35 WORDS FOR SUCCESS

Match the sentences on the left with the sentences on the right.
Write the correct number on each line. Each number can be used more
than once.

WHAT TO DO

1. Say the name of the person you networked with and your relationship to that person.

2. Ask about job openings.

WHAT TO SAY

_1_ My friend, Karen Shain, told me to call you.

___ She told me that you may have some job openings in your company.

___ She said that you might know about some job openings.

___ I got your telephone number from my neighbor, Joan Hopkins.

36 LISTENING

You will hear Sonia, a job applicant, making a networking follow-up phone call. Fill in the blanks.

Sonia: Hi. My name is Sonia Chang. _____, Mario Martinez,

_____.

Anna: Oh, Mario. How is he?

Sonia: Good. I'm calling because I _____ a job as a waitress.

Anna: Uh-huh.

Sonia: He said that _____ have some _____ in your restaurant.

Anna: Well, actually, I think we need a waitress now. Could you call back tomorrow?

Sonia: Sure. _____.

Anna: You're welcome. Goodbye.

Sonia: Goodbye.

37 PAIR WORK

Work with a partner. Practice the conversation in Exercise 36. When you finish, change roles.

38 ROLE PLAYS

INFORMATION GAP: Student A, look at this page. Student B, look at page 212.

Work with a partner. Read the first situation. Then create a conversation. When you finish, read the second situation. Create another conversation.

1. Student A, you are looking for a job as (your job goal). A few days ago, you networked with your friend, and your friend told you to call Student B. You do not know Student B. Call Student B and network.

2. Student A, you do not know Student B. Student B is looking for a job. Student B calls you. Tell Student B about a job opening in your company.

39 ON YOUR OWN: Your Network

Who is in your network? Write the names of the people in your network.

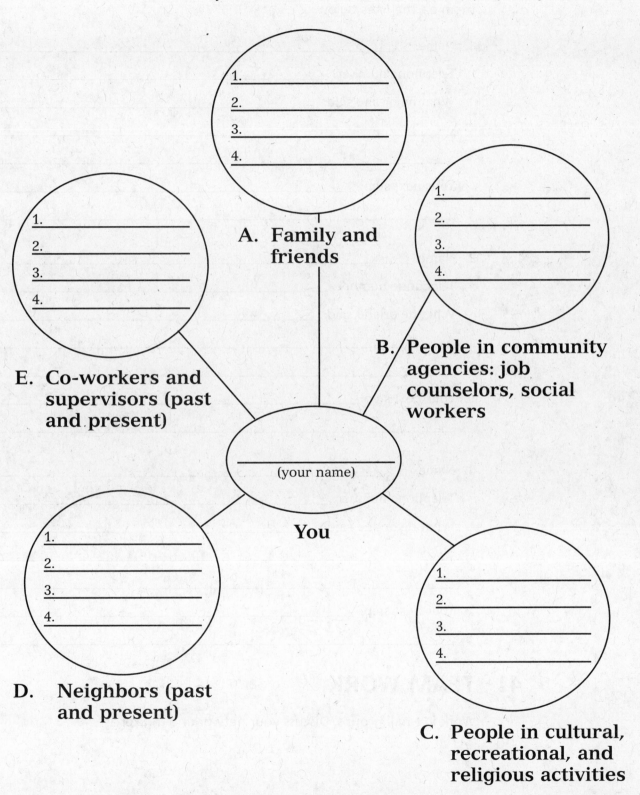

A. Family and friends

1. _____
2. _____
3. _____
4. _____

1. _____
2. _____
3. _____
4. _____

E. Co-workers and supervisors (past and present)

1. _____
2. _____
3. _____
4. _____

B. People in community agencies: job counselors, social workers

_____
(your name)

You

1. _____
2. _____
3. _____
4. _____

D. Neighbors (past and present)

1. _____
2. _____
3. _____
4. _____

C. People in cultural, recreational, and religious activities

40 APPLY YOURSELF

Talk to three people in your network. Then write the information about them on the lines below.

1. Name: _____

   Telephone number: _____

   What he or she said: _____

   _____

   _____

   Your next step: _____

   _____

2. Name: _____

   Telephone number: _____

   What he or she said: _____

   _____

   _____

   Your next step: _____

   _____

3. Name: _____

   Telephone number: _____

   What he or she said: _____

   _____

   _____

   Your next step: _____

   _____

41 TEAM WORK

Work in small groups. Discuss your networking in Exercise 40.

WHAT DO YOU THINK NOW?

Discuss these questions with your classmates.

1. When you walk into a company to ask about job openings, what should you say to the receptionist?
   What should you say to the manager?

2. Your body language and your personal appearance are very important when you meet a manager. What should you do? What shouldn't you do?

3. What job information can you find out from a want ad?

4. Who do people network with in this country?

5. What do many people think is the best way to find a job in this country?

42 REVIEW: Cooperative Crossword Puzzle

INFORMATION GAP: Student A, look at this page. Student B, look at page 213.

There are two different clues for each word. Read your clue to your partner. Listen to your partner's clue. Then choose the correct word from the list. Write it in the spaces.

EXAMPLE: Student A: #1 Down. "You can send your resume with this machine."

Student B: #1 Down. "This machine has a number like a telephone number."

ABBREVIATION
ANNOUNCEMENTS
APPLICATION
BODY LANGUAGE
DUTIES
EXPERIENCE
✔ FAX
HELP WANTED
MANAGER
NETWORKING
OPENINGS
PREFERRED
RESUME
WANT ADS
WALK IN

ACROSS CLUES

2. This is good when you stand straight and look at the manager's face.
6. The work you did in your past jobs.
8. These have the same information as want ads.
10. You can ask for this when you walk into a company.
11. Helpful, desired, a plus.
12. Job announcements in a newspaper.
14. These are positions for new workers in a company.
15. You can give this document to managers and to people in your network.

DOWN CLUES

1. You can send your resume with this machine.
3. Sometimes this is the first few letters of a word.
4. A sign you can see in a store or a restaurant window.
5. Supervisor, boss.
7. Many people think this is the best way to find a job in the United States.
9. To go into a company and ask for a job.
13. Work you will do at a job.

UNIT 3

Calling about a Job: Leaving a Message

WHAT DO YOU THINK?

Discuss these questions with your classmates.

1. When you call a company about a job, who will you talk to?

2. If you call a company and hear a recorded message, what should you do? What should you say?

3. If you call and talk to a receptionist or another employee, what should you say?

4. Why is it more difficult to understand someone on the telephone than in a face-to-face conversation?

In this unit, you will:

- Learn how to use the telephone when you are looking for a job.

- Learn how to leave a message on an answering machine or on voice mail.

- Learn how to leave a message with a receptionist or another employee.

LEAVING A MESSAGE ON AN ANSWERING MACHINE OR VOICE MAIL

When you call a business to find out about a job, sometimes you will not hear a person. Sometimes you will hear a message on an answering machine or voice mail. An answering machine is a machine that can take telephone messages when someone is not at home or in an office. Many businesses have voice mail. Voice mail is like an answering machine. It is a system that takes messages for people when they cannot answer the telephone. It is important to listen carefully to the recorded message because it will tell you what you should do next.

⌒ 1 LISTENING

You will hear four telephone messages. What does each message tell you to do? Write the number of the conversation next to the correct answer.

___ Wait. Someone will talk to you soon.

___ You can talk to someone if you press "O," or you can leave a message.

___ The business is closed. You need to call again.

___ Leave a message, and someone will call you later.

Now turn to p. 214 and read the messages that you just listened to and check your answers. Try to understand the main idea even if you do not understand every word.

2 WORDS FOR SUCCESS

Read the messages on page 214 again. Then look at the underlined words in the following exercise. What do the underlined words mean? Circle the correct letter.

1. You've <u>reached</u> the Acme Company means
   a. this is the Acme Company.
   b. you need to hang up and call later.

2. <u>Business hours</u> are
   a. the time when a place is open.
   b. the time when a place is closed.

3. When you <u>call back</u>, you
   a. call a different number.
   b. call again.

4. The Acme Company's <u>regular office hours</u> start at
   a. 8:00 in the morning.
   b. 5:00 in the afternoon.

5. When nobody can <u>take your call</u>, no one can
   a. talk to you.
   b. call you.

6. <u>We'll return your call</u> means someone will
   a. take your call now.
   b. call you later.

7. <u>You'd like to be connected</u> means
   a. you want to talk to someone.
   b. you want someone to call you.

8. When you hear "<u>press zero</u>," you need to
   a. call back later.
   b. push the zero on the telephone.

9. <u>Someone will be right with you</u> means someone will
   a. call you back.
   b. talk to you soon.

10. <u>Currently</u> means
    a. right now.
    b. in a short time.

11. When you hear, "<u>please hold</u>," you need to
    a. wait.
    b. call later.

12. <u>Shortly</u> and <u>as soon as possible</u> mean
    a. right now.
    b. in a short time.

HOW TO LEAVE A MESSAGE ON AN ANSWERING MACHINE

When you leave a message about a job on an answering machine, you need to do these things:

- Say your first name, then your last name.
- Spell your last name.
- Say what job you are looking for.
- Tell how you found out about the job.
- Say your telephone number.
- Say thank you.

3 WORDS FOR SUCCESS

Match the sentences on the left with the sentences on the right. Write the correct number on each line. Each number can be used more than once.

WHAT TO DO

1. Introduce yourself.

2. Spell your last name.

3. Say what job you are looking for.

4. Tell how you found out about the job.

5. Say your telephone number.

6. Say thank you.

WHAT TO SAY

___ My telephone number is . . .

_1_ My name is . . .

___ I'm calling about the job as . . .

___ I saw your ad in the (newspaper).

___ That's spelled S–H–A–I–N.

___ This is . . .

___ (Name) told me that you have a job opening.

___ That's S–H–A–I–N.

___ My number is . . .

___ I'm interested in the job as . . .

___ Thank you very much.

___ I saw your job listing at the State Employment Agency.

___ Thank you.

⌢ 4 LISTENING

You will hear three people leaving messages. What does each person say? Check (✔) the correct column.

	1	2	3
This is . . .			
My name is . . .			
That's spelled . . .			
That's . . .			
I'm calling about the job as . . .			
I'm interested in the job as . . .			
I saw your ad in the (newspaper).			
I saw your job listing at (place).			
(Name) told me that you have a job opening.			
My telephone number is . . .			
My number is . . .			
Thank you.			

⌢ 5 LISTENING

Listen again to the messages in Exercise 4. Discuss these questions with your classmates.

1. In which conversations did the caller forget something?
2. What did he or she forget?

LANGUAGE FOCUS
Spelling your Name

Your last name may be simple (Lee), or it may be difficult (Chafcouloff), but it is always important to spell your last name when you leave a message on an answering machine or voice mail. When you spell your name, the person who receives your message can write and say your name correctly.

Two rules will help you spell your name clearly on the telephone:

Rule 1: Spell with rhythm: Say three or four letters at one time, then pause.

My last name is Chafcouloff.
That's C–H–A–F / C–O–U / L–O–F–F.

Rule 2: Some letters are difficult to understand on the telephone (B, D, G, P, V). You can use "code names" to make your spelling clear.

My last name is Delgado.
That's D–E–L / G as in George / A–D–O.

Here are some "code names" you can use:

B as in Betty	N as in Nancy
C as in Carol	P as in Peter
D as in David	R as in Robert
F as in Frank	S as in Susan
G as in George	T as in Thomas
H as in Harry	V as in Victor
J as in Judy	W as in Wendy
L as in Lisa	Z as in Zebra
M as in Mary	

BE CAREFUL: Use only one or two code names.

6 LISTENING

You will hear four people spelling their names. Listen and write the last names.

1. _____

2. _____

3. _____

4. _____

7 ON YOUR OWN

Write your last name. Use the rules in the Language Focus box so you can spell your name clearly on the telephone. Write three or four letters. Then leave a space. Use code names for the letters that are the most difficult to understand.

Your last name: _____

8 TEAM WORK

Work in small groups. Ask three of your classmates for their names. Then ask your classmates to spell their last names. Ask questions when you don't understand the spelling. Write your classmates' last names. When you finish, check your spelling with your classmates.

EXAMPLE:

Student A: Could you tell me your name, please?

Student B: My name is Jesse Arguello.

Student A: Could you spell your last name, please?

Student B: Sure. That's A–R–G as in George / U–E / L–L–O.

1. _____

2. _____

3. _____

9 ON YOUR OWN

You are calling about a job that you want (your short-term goal). You hear an answering machine or voice mail message. What will you say? Write the message you will leave.

Hello. This is _____

(your first name, then your last name)

That's _____

(spell your last name)

I'm calling about the job as _____

(your short-term job goal)

_____

(how you found out about the job)

My telephone number is _____

(your telephone number)

10 TEAM WORK

Work in small groups. Take turns reading your messages in Exercise 9. Be enthusiastic! Did you understand your classmates' messages? Did they sound enthusiastic?

YOUR ANSWERING MACHINE OR VOICE MAIL MESSAGE

After you leave a message for a manager, the manager may call you back. This can be a problem if you do not have an answering machine at your home. For example, maybe you will not be home when a manager calls you, or maybe other people in your house do not speak English.

It is a good idea to have an answering machine at home. If you get an answering machine for your home, you need to record an outgoing message (the message people will hear when they call your answering machine).

Here are two examples of messages you can record on your home answering machine:

EXAMPLE 1: Hello. This is (your telephone number). We are not at home now. Please leave a message after the tone, and we'll call you back as soon as possible.

EXAMPLE 2: Hello. This is (your first and last name). I'm sorry. I can't come to the phone now. Please leave a message after the beep. Thank you.

11 ON YOUR OWN

Write the message you will record on your home answering machine.

_____

_____

_____

_____

12 TEAM WORK

Work in small groups. Practice your home answering machine message with your classmates. Did you understand your classmates' messages?

CULTURE NOTES
Tips for Telephoning

The telephone is very important in North America. In some countries, people usually go to see a person when they want to talk. In North America, people usually use the telephone when they want to talk because it is faster and easier. Almost everyone has a telephone at home. Most people have home answering machines or voice mail. In business, people use the telephone every day.

When you are looking for a job, sometimes you need to use the telephone. When you find out about a job, you should call as soon as possible. It is important to know how to be polite on the telephone and how to leave a good telephone message.

Here are some things to remember about using the telephone.

Before you make a telephone call:
- Prepare and practice what you will say.
- You can write down what you want to say and read it on the phone. The receptionist and the manager can't see you!

When you can't talk to the person you are calling:
- Don't hang up! Always leave a message.
- Leave a short message.
- Remember that a manager can be a man or a woman. If you are not sure, ask the receptionist, "Is that Mr. or Ms.?"

When you are talking on the telephone:
- Speak slowly and clearly.
- Be confident. Don't speak very softly. Don't sound nervous.
- Be friendly and enthusiastic! Put a smile in your voice.
- Listen carefully to what someone tells you or asks you.
- Don't interrupt. Don't talk when someone is talking to you.

13 TEAM WORK

Work in small groups. Discuss these questions with your classmates.

1. In your country, when do people usually use the telephone?
   Do people use the telephone for business?
   Do people have long conversations with their friends on the telephone?

2. Why do you need to prepare and practice what you will say before you make a telephone call?
   Why is it a good idea to write down what you will say?

3. Why do you need to call a business immediately when you find out about a job?

4. In your country, do you usually leave messages on answering machines or with receptionists?
   Why do you need to leave a short message on an answering machine or with a receptionist?

5. Why is it important to be friendly and enthusiastic when you talk to a receptionist?

14 ON YOUR OWN

What should you do when you talk on the telephone? What shouldn't you do? Write sentences, using the phrases in the box.

> ✔ listen carefully   speak very fast
> practice before you call   be friendly
> ask, "Is that Mr. or Ms.?"   speak very softly
> ✔ hang up if the manager isn't there   speak clearly
> leave a long message   interrupt
> be enthusiastic

Dos

1. _You should listen carefully._

2. _____

3. _____

4. _____

5. _____

6. _____

Don'ts

1. _You shouldn't hang up if the manager isn't there._

2. _____

3. _____

4. _____

5. _____

15 TEAM WORK

Work in small groups. Compare your answers in Exercise 14. Can you think of any other things you should or shouldn't do when you talk on the telephone?

INTRODUCING YOURSELF TO A RECEPTIONIST

When you call a business to find out about a job, you want to talk to the manager, but the manager does not usually answer the telephone. The first person you talk to is usually the receptionist or another employee. You need to introduce yourself to this person.

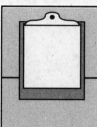

HOW TO INTRODUCE YOURSELF TO A RECEPTIONIST

When you talk to a receptionist, you need to do these things:

- Say your first name, then your last name.
- Say what job you are looking for.
- Tell how you found out about the job.
- Ask to speak to the manager.

After you introduce yourself, three possible things can happen:

- The receptionist will connect you to the manager.

  or

- The receptionist will not connect you to the manager because the manager is busy or out of the office.

  or

- The receptionist will ask you to wait. He or she will find out if the manager can talk to you.

🎧 16 LISTENING

You will hear eight people calling about jobs and talking to receptionists. If the receptionist will connect the caller to the manager, check (✔) *Yes*. If the receptionist will not connect the caller to the manager, check (✔) *No*. If you do not know, check (✔) *?*.

	1	2	3	4	5	6	7	8
Yes								
No								
?								

17 WORDS FOR SUCCESS

Match the sentences on the left with the sentences on the right.
Write the correct number on each line. Each number can be used
more than once.

WHAT THE RECEPTIONIST WILL DO

1. The receptionist will connect you.

2. The receptionist will not connect you.

3. The receptionist will ask you to wait.

WHAT THE RECEPTIONIST WILL SAY

<u>1</u> Just a minute. I'll connect you.

___ Please hold.

___ She's in a meeting right now.

___ I'm sorry. He's not in.

___ She's away from her desk.

___ I'll see if he's in.

___ Sure. Just a moment, please.

___ I'll see if he's available.

LEAVING A MESSAGE WITH A RECEPTIONIST

When you call about a job, you need to tell the receptionist information about yourself. This is the same information you say to the receptionist when you walk into a company. Then you need to ask for the manager. If you cannot talk to the manager, you need to leave a message with the receptionist. You can leave the same message that you leave on an answering machine or voice mail, but you do *not* need to spell your name. Spell your name only when the receptionist asks you to.

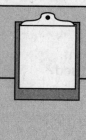

HOW TO LEAVE A MESSAGE WITH A RECEPTIONIST

If the manager is not in, you need to do these things:

- Ask for the manager's name.
- Ask how to spell the manager's name.
- Ask when the manager will be in.
- Leave a message (your name, telephone number, and the reason you are calling).
- Say thank you.

18 WORDS FOR SUCCESS

Match the sentences on the left with the sentences on the right.
Write the correct number on each line. Each number can be used more than once.

WHAT TO DO

1. Ask for the manager's name.

2. Ask how to spell the manager's name.

3. Ask when the manager will be in.

4. Ask to leave a message.

5. Leave a message.

WHAT TO SAY

_3_ May I leave a message, please?

___ Please tell the manager that I called and that I am very interested in the job as . . .

___ May I have the manager's name, please?

___ Could you take a message, please?

___ Could you tell me when the manager will be in, please?

___ My name is . . ., and I'm interested in the job as . . .

___ Could you spell that, please?

___ Could you tell me the manager's name, please?

⌒ 19 LISTENING

You will hear three people calling about jobs and talking to receptionists. What does each caller do? Check (✔) the correct boxes.

	1	2	3
Asks for the manager's name			
Asks how to spell the manager's name			
Asks when the manager will be in			
Asks to leave a message			
Leaves a message			

⌒ 20 LISTENING

Listen again to the conversations in Exercise 19. Then discuss these questions with your classmates.

1. In which conversations did the caller forget something?

2. What did he or she forget?

⌒ 21 LISTENING

You will hear three people talking to receptionists. What is the manager's name in each conversation? Write the manager's last names. Circle *Mr.* or *Ms.*

1. Mr. / Ms. _____

2. Mr. / Ms. _____

3. Mr. / Ms. _____

22 PAIR WORK

Complete the applicant's part of the conversation, using the sentences in the box. Then practice the conversation with a partner.

> Could you spell that, please?
> ✔ May I speak to the person who does the hiring, please?
> Thank you.
> Lily Tai. Could you tell me when she will be in, please?
> Please tell her that Roberto Ortiz called, and that I'm interested in the job as a painter. My telephone number is 648-4679.
> Could I leave a message, please?
> Could you tell me her name, please?

Receptionist: Good morning, Tai Painting Services. May I help you?

Applicant: Hello. This is Roberto Ortiz. I'm calling about a job as a painter. My friend, Walter Chien, told me you have a job opening.
May I speak to the person who does the hiring, please?

Receptionist: I'm sorry. She's not available now.

Applicant: _____

Receptionist: Sure. It's Lily Tai.

Applicant: _____

Receptionist: Yes. It's Lily Tai. That's T as in Thomas, A–I.

Applicant: _____

Receptionist: She'll be in at 3:00 this afternoon.

Applicant: _____

Receptionist: Certainly. What should I tell Ms. Tai?

Applicant: _____

_____

Receptionist: Okay, Mr. Ortiz. I'll give her the message.

Applicant: _____

Receptionist: You're welcome. Goodbye.

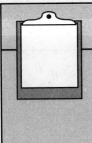

QUESTIONS A RECEPTIONIST CAN ASK YOU

When you call about a job, you might forget to tell the receptionist important information. Then the receptionist will ask you some questions. He or she might ask you:

- Your name
- Who you want to talk to
- Why you are calling
- If you want to leave a message

23 ON YOUR OWN

Here are some questions a receptionist can ask you when you call a business about a job. Write the different ways to ask the same question, using the questions in the box.

> What is this regarding?
> ✔ Could I have your name, please?
> Who's calling, please?
> Who would you like to speak with?
> How can I help you?
> Would you like to leave a message?
> How should I direct your call?
> May I ask who's calling?
> Could I take a message?
> What are you calling about?
> Who should I say is calling?

1. What's your name?

   a. _Could I have your name, please?_

   b. _____

   c. _____

   d. _____

2. Who do you want to talk to?

   a. _____

   b. _____

3. Why are you calling?

   a. _____

   b. _____

   c. _____

4. Do you want to leave a message?

   a. _____

   b. _____

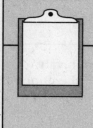

INFORMATION A RECEPTIONIST CAN TELL YOU

The receptionist can also tell you some information. She or he may tell you:

- Come in and fill out an application.
- Send a resume.
- There are no jobs.
- Call again.

24 ON YOUR OWN

Here is some information a receptionist can tell you when you call a business about a job. Write the different ways to say the same information, using the sentences in the box.

> There are no positions available now.
> ✔ Could you call at 2:00?
> Could you come in and fill out an application?
> That position is filled.
> We're no longer accepting applications.
> Could you call back later?
> Why don't you fax us your resume?
> Can you try again tomorrow?
> Would you like to come in and fill out an application?
> Could you send your resume?

1. Call again.

    a. <u>Could you call at 2:00?</u>

    b. _____

    c. _____

2. There are no jobs.

    a. _____

    b. _____

    c. _____

3. Come to our office and fill out an application.

    a. _____

    b. _____

4. Send your resume.

    a. _____

    b. _____

🎧 25 LISTENING

You will hear a receptionist say a sentence. What should a job applicant say next? Circle the correct letter.

1. a. I'm calling about the job as a copy machine operator.
    b. Sure. Could you tell me your address, please?
    c. I want to work as a copy machine operator. Call me at 222-1087.
    d. Should I call back tomorrow?

2. a. My telephone number is 703-0734.
    b. I'm interested in a job as a computer technician.
    c. Could you tell me her name, please?
    d. Could I send my resume to you anyway?

3. a. Sure. Could you tell me when he will be in, please?
    b. Could you spell that, please?
    c. I saw your ad in the *Post*.
    d. May I speak to the manager, please?

4. a. I'm calling about the job as a clerk.
    b. This is Karen Matthews.
    c. Could I speak to the person who does the hiring, please?
    d. Call me at 397-4219.

5. a. Yes. Could you tell me when the manager will be in, please?
    b. Fine. Could you spell the manager's name, please?
    c. Okay, I'll send my resume tomorrow. Thank you very much.
    d. Could I fill out an application anyway?

6. a. Could I leave a message, please?
    b. Could I talk to the person who does the hiring, please?
    c. Could you tell me your address, please?
    d. My name is Pat Zody, and I'm calling about the job as a child care worker.

7. a. May I leave a message, please?
    b. Will there be any openings in the future?
    c. Yes, I would like to fill out an application.
    d. I saw your ad in the *Register*.

8. a. This is Jim Bell. Could I speak to the personnel manager, please?
    b. Yes. Please tell the manager that Jim Bell called, and I'm interested in the job as a baker's assistant.
    c. I'm calling about a job as a baker's assistant. Do you have any jobs?
    d. Yes. Could I leave a message, please?

26 PAIR WORK

Create a conversation with a partner. Student A is a receptionist and says the sentences on the left. Student B is a job applicant and follows the directions on the right. Ask questions when you do not understand. When you finish, change roles.

RECEPTIONIST	APPLICANT
1. Hello. May I help you?	→ 1. Introduce yourself, and ask to speak to the manager.
2. I'm sorry. The manager is not in.	→ 2. Ask if you can leave a message.
3. Certainly.	→ 3. Leave a message.
4. Could you spell your last name, please?	→ 4. Spell your last name.
5. Thank you.	→ 5. Ask for the manager's name.
6. Chris Treadway.	→ 6. Ask how to spell the manager's name.
7. T–R–E/A–D/W–A–Y.	→ 7. Thank the receptionist. Ask if it is Mr. or Ms.
8. It's Ms. Treadway.	→ 8. Repeat the name. Ask when to call back.
9. Tuesday morning.	→ 9. Repeat the time and say thank you.
10. You're welcome. Goodbye.	→ 10. Say goodbye.

27 REVIEW: Problem Solving

PART A

Work with a partner. Read about three callers who did not leave good telephone messages on answering machines. What mistakes did each caller make?

1. Peter Wagner called about a job as a warehouse worker. He left a message on the manager's answering machine. He said, "Hello. My name is Peter. That's P–E–T/E–R. I'm interested in a job. I saw your job listing at Boston University. My telephone number is (617) 786-3297."

2. Alvina Medina saw an ad in the *Journal* about a job as a gardener. Alvina left a voice mail message for the personnel manager, Robin Eisenberg. Alvina was enthusiastic, and she spoke very fast. Alvina said, "Hello. This is a message for Mr. Eisenberg. My name is Alvina Medina. That's M–E–D/I–N–A. I'm calling about the job as a gardener. My telephone number is (414) 647-3972. Thank you."

3. Rita Krupnik called Mount Zion Hospital about a job as a laboratory assistant. Her friend, Mahasen Ajlan, had told her about a job opening there. She heard an answering machine and said, "Hello. My name is Rita Krupnik. I'm interested in the job as a laboratory assistant. Thank you very much. Goodbye."

PART B

Work with a partner. Read about two callers who talked to receptionists. What mistakes did each caller make?

4. Thea Sonnemans saw an advertisement in the *Herald* for a job as a sales clerk at a store. Two weeks later, Thea called the store and talked to a receptionist in the personnel department.

   Receptionist: Hello. May I help you?

   Thea: Hello. My name is Thea Sonnemans. I'm calling about the job as a sales clerk.

   Receptionist: I'm sorry. That position is filled, but you can come in and fill out an application at our store when you have time.

   Thea: Oh. Thank you. Goodbye.

5. Robert Griffiths called the Sutro Company about a job as a computer technician. His friend, Penn Garvin, had told him about a job opening there. He talked to a receptionist.

   Receptionist: Sutro Company. May I help you?

   Robert: Hello. I want the personnel manager.

   Receptionist: She's away from her desk. Would you like to leave a message?

   Robert: No. I'll call back. What's his name?

   Receptionist: Ms. Chakalian.

   Robert: What? Oh . . . Goodbye.

28 ON YOUR OWN

You are calling a business about a job that you want. A receptionist or another employee answers the phone. What will you say? Write your introduction.

My name is _____

(your first name, then your last name)

I'm interested in the job as _____

(your short-term goal)

_____

(how you found out about the job)

Could I speak to the manager, please?

29 ROLE PLAYS

INFORMATION GAP: Student A, look at this page. Student B, look at page 214.

Work with a partner. Read the first situation. Then create a conversation. When you finish, read the second situation. Create another conversation.

1. Student A, you are the receptionist at Projects International. Student B is a job applicant. The personnel manager, Griff Williams, is in a meeting. He will be available at 10:00 tomorrow morning. Take a message. Use the message form below. Remember to write down the name, the telephone number, and the job.

P H O N E M E M O	TO		DATE	TIME	AM
					PM
	FROM		PHONE NO.		
	M E S S A G E				

2. Student A, you are a job applicant. Student B is a receptionist. You are looking for a job as (your job goal). You call the Fuller Company. Introduce yourself. Remember to ask for the manager's name and a good time to call back. Leave a good message. Ask questions if you do not understand. Write down all important information.

Notes: Manager's name: _____

_____

When to call back: _____

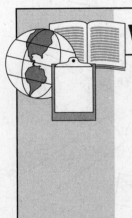

WHAT DO YOU THINK NOW?

Discuss these questions with your classmates.

1. If you call a company and hear a recorded message, what should you do? What should you say?

2. If you are calling about a job and you talk to a receptionist or another employee, what should you say?

3. When you are talking on the telephone, what are some things you should do? What are some things you shouldn't do?

30 REVIEW: Game

Listen to your teacher's instructions. Then play the game.

PART A

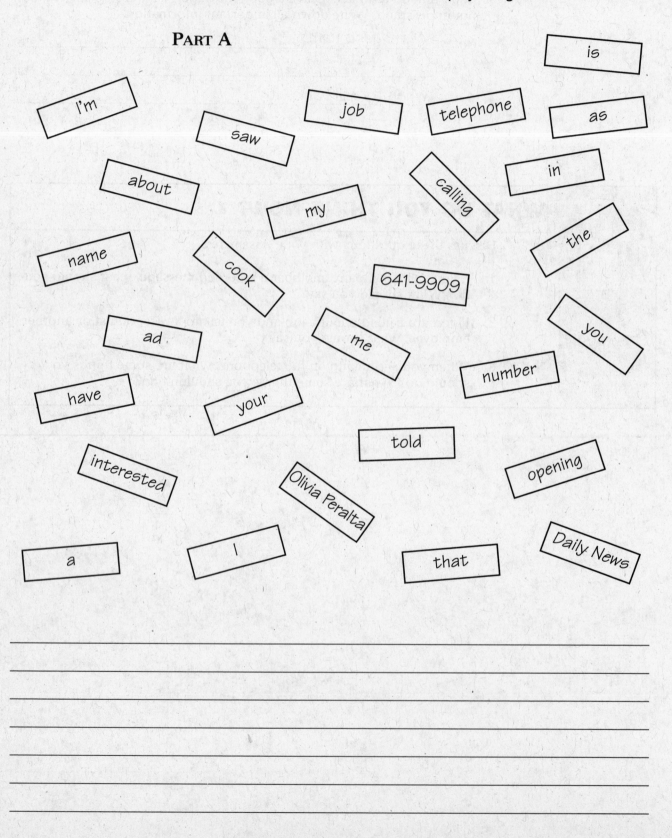

is

I'm

job   telephone   as

saw

about   calling   in

my

the

name   cook   641-9909

ad   me   you

number

have   your

told

interested   opening

Olivia Peralta

a   I   that   Daily News

_____

_____

_____

_____

_____

_____

PART B

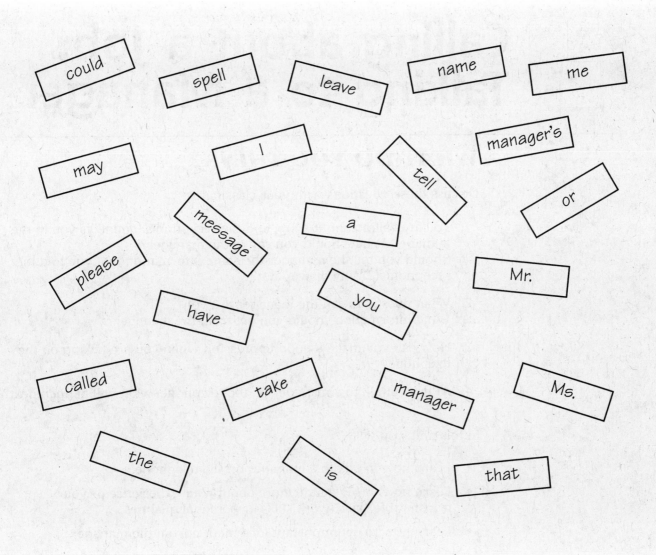

_____

_____

_____

_____

_____

_____

UNIT 4

Calling about a Job: Talking to a Manager

WHAT DO YOU THINK?

Discuss these questions with your classmates.

1. You are calling about a job, and the receptionist connects you to the manager. What should you say to the manager?
   Should you tell the manager the same information that you told the receptionist? Why or why not?

2. What questions can the manager ask you?
   What information should you get from the manager?

3. How can you make a good impression when you are talking on the telephone?

4. After you talk to a manager on the telephone, what will happen next?

In this unit, you will:

- Learn how to talk to a manager on the telephone.

- Learn how to say a little more about your experience or your transferable skills (work skills or personal qualities).

- Learn how to get important information from the manager.

INTRODUCING YOURSELF TO A MANAGER

After you introduce yourself to the receptionist on the telephone, you need to introduce yourself again to the manager. You need to tell the manager the same information that you told the receptionist. Then you also need to tell the manager how many years' experience you have, or a little about your transferable skills. This is the same information that you say to the manager when you walk into a company to apply for a job.

⌒ 1 LISTENING

Carlos Paz is calling about a job. Read the questions. Then listen to the conversation. Circle the correct letter or letters.

1. What job is Carlos calling about?

   a. electronics technician
   b. office clerk
   c. copy machine operator

2. What does Carlos tell the receptionist?

   a. his name and the job he is calling about
   b. how he found out about the job
   c. about his experience

3. How did Carlos find out about the job?

   a. networking
   b. want ads
   c. walking in

4. What does Carlos tell the manager?

   a. his name and the job he is calling about
   b. how he found out about the job
   c. about his experience

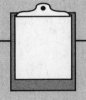

HOW TO INTRODUCE YOURSELF TO A MANAGER

When you first talk to a manager, you need to do these things:

- Say your first name, then your last name.
- Say what job you are looking for.
- Tell how you found out about the job.

When you have past experience in the job you want now, you also need to do these things:

- Say your past job title.
- Say how many years' experience you have.

When you do *not* have past experience in the job you want now, or when you do not have any work experience, you also need to do this:

- Tell the manager one or two of your transferable skills.

After you tell the manager about your experience or your skills, you need to do this:

- Say that you are interested in the job.

2 PAIR WORK

Work with a partner. Read the situations. What should each applicant say to the manager? Look at the example.

EXAMPLE: Rosa Rivera is looking for a job as a child care worker. She was a housewife and has three children. She loves to take care of children. She can also drive a car. She networked with her neighbor, Robert Roth. Robert told her about a job opening as a child care worker. He told Rosa to call his friend, Lucia Hernandez, who is looking for a person with child care and driving experience. Rosa is going to call about the job. What should she say to Lucia?

Hello. This is Rosa Rivera. I'm calling about the job as a child care worker. My neighbor, Robert Roth, told me that you have a job opening. I have three children, and I can take care of children very well. I can also drive a car, and I'm a very good driver. I'm really interested in this job.

1. Kin Phan was a computer technician for ten years. He saw this want ad in the *Sentinel*. Kin is going to call about the job. What should he say to the manager?

Computer Technician. F/T. Exper. req. Exc. benes. Call Sarah betw. 10 and 12. 753-872.

2. Marco Martinez worked as a carpenter and construction worker for five years. In his last job, Marco moved heavy equipment and supplies. He is very strong and friendly. Marco saw this job listing at the State Employment Agency. He is going to call about the job. What should he say to the manager?

JOB LISTING:	POSITION AVAILABLE
Title:	Baggage Porter
Description:	To work at large hotel: carry hand baggage, take guests to rooms, move heavy baggage.
Requirements:	Must be able to lift heavy baggage. Must work well with others. No experience necessary.
Salary:	$6.50 per hour.
How to apply:	Call Roman at 657-5284.

_____

_____

_____

_____

_____

3. Serge McKenzie was a librarian for two years. He is organized, and he knows a lot about books. He networked with his friend, Andrew Blaskey. Andrew told him about a job as a cashier in a bookstore. Andrew told him to call the manager, Jerry Ochoa. What should he say to the manager?

_____

_____

_____

_____

_____

TELLING A MANAGER MORE ABOUT YOURSELF

After you introduce yourself, the manager will often ask you to say more about yourself or more about your experience. The manager wants to know a little more about you before he or she asks you to come to a job interview. If you have experience in the type of job you are calling about, talk more about your experience. If you don't have experience, talk more about your transferable skills.

⌂ 3 LISTENING

You will hear four applicants calling about jobs and talking to managers. Does each applicant have past work experience in the job he or she is calling about? Circle *Yes* or *No*.

Caller #1	Yes	No
Caller #2	Yes	No
Caller #3	Yes	No
Caller #4	Yes	No

HOW TO TELL A MANAGER MORE ABOUT YOURSELF

When you have past work experience in the job you want, you need to tell the manager:

- Some of your past job duties or work skills

EXAMPLE: *Past job*: Painter   *Job goal*: Painter

"I was a painter. In my last job, I painted inside and outside apartments and offices. I removed paint from walls. I used paint brushes and ladders."

When you do <u>not</u> have past work experience in the job you want, you need to tell the manager:

- More about your transferable skills—some examples of your work skills, life skills, or personal qualities that will be useful for this job

and / or

- About your education: courses you took or certificates you have that will be helpful for this job

EXAMPLE: *Past job*: Travel agent   *Job goal*: Driver

"In my last job, I was a travel agent. I can read maps, and I can drive very well. I'm friendly, and I'm very reliable."

EXAMPLE: *Past job*: Nurse   *Job goal*: Cosmetology assistant

"I was a nurse in my country. In the United States, I studied cosmetology for eight months, and now I have a certificate. I work well with people."

4 WORDS FOR SUCCESS

Match the sentences on the left with the sentences on the right.
Write the correct number on each line. Each number can be used
more than once.

WHAT TO DO

1. Say your past job title.

2. Talk about your past job duties.

3. Talk about your skills.

4. Talk about your personal qualities.

5. Talk about your education.

WHAT TO SAY

___ I'm studying refrigeration repair.

___ I know how to drive a car.

___ I studied computers at a technical college.

___ I am energetic.

___ In my last job, I repaired televisions and radios.

_1_ I was a farmer.

___ I work well under pressure.

___ I can cut and style hair.

___ I have a certificate in nursing.

___ When I was a baggage porter, I took guests to their rooms and carried baggage.

___ I worked as a carpenter.

5 LISTENING

You will hear three applicants calling about jobs and talking to
managers. What does each caller say? Check (✔) the correct column.

	1	2	3
In my last job, I . . .			
When I was a/an . . . , I . . .			
I am . . .			
I can . . .			
I know how to . . .			
I'm studying . . .			
I studied . . .			
I have a certificate . . .			

6 ON YOUR OWN

You call about a job and you are connected to a manager. When you first talk to the manager, what will you say? If the manager asks you to say more about yourself or your experience, what will you say? Write your answers.

Manager: Geri Kahn. How can I help you?

You: Hello. My name is _____
                                    (your first name, then your last name)

             I'm calling about the job as _____
                                             (your short-term job goal)

             _____
                         (how you found out about the job)

             _____
                 (one sentence about your experience or transferable skills)

Manager: Could you tell me more about your experience?

You: _____

             _____

             _____

             _____

7 PAIR WORK

Work with a partner. Practice the conversation in Exercise 6. The applicant should be enthusiastic. When you finish, change roles.

CULTURE NOTES
More Tips for Telephoning

Talking to a manager on the telephone is only the first step in getting a job. Most managers will not give you a job after a telephone conversation. It is important to meet the manager and to talk to the manager face-to-face. You want to make a good impression on the telephone so the manager will ask you to come in for an interview.

BE CAREFUL: Sometimes a manager wants to save time, and he or she will try to interview you on the telephone. This is not good for you because you can make a better impression in a face-to-face interview. If the manager asks you many questions, you can say, "Excuse me, could I make an appointment for an interview?"

Here are some ways to make a good impression on the telephone.

Be professional:

- Talk only about your experience and skills.
- Do not talk about your family or about why you need a job.

Be an active listener; do not be silent:

- When the manager tells you some information and you understand, say "Uh-huh," "Okay," or "I see" to show him/her that you are listening.
- When the manager asks you a question, say something immediately. Say "Let me think" or "Well . . . " when you understand the question but you need time to think.
- When the manager tells you some information or asks you a question and you don't understand, ask the manager to repeat the information or to speak more slowly.
- When you want to write down information that the manager tells you, say "Just a second, I'm writing this down."

8 TEAM WORK

Work in small groups. Discuss these questions.

1. Why isn't it a good idea to talk about your family or your personal life when you are talking to the manager?

2. What will a manager think if an applicant says, "I really need this job!"?

3. What will a manager think if he or she pauses (stops talking) or asks a question, and you don't say anything?

4. In your country, what do you say on the telephone to show that you are listening?

9 ON YOUR OWN

What should you do when you talk to a manager on the telephone? What shouldn't you do? Write sentences, using the phrases in the box.

> ✔ ask the manager to speak slowly if you do not understand
> ✔ talk about your family
>   have an interview on the telephone
>   be silent when you don't understand
>   say "Uh-huh," or "I see" to show you are listening
>   say a little about your experience and skills
>   tell the manager why you really need a job
>   say "Let me think" when the manager asks a difficult question
>   write down information that the manager tells you

Dos

1. You should ask the manager to speak slowly if you do not understand.

2. _____

3. _____

4. _____

5. _____

Don'ts

1. You should not talk about your family.

2. _____

3. _____

4. _____

10 TEAM WORK

Work in small groups. Compare your answers in Exercise 9. Are they the same or different? Can you think of any other things that you should or shouldn't do when you talk to a manager on the telephone?

🎧 11   LISTENING

You will hear three applicants calling about jobs and talking to managers. Do you think each applicant makes a good impression? Circle *Yes* or *No*.

Caller #1	Yes	No
Caller #2	Yes	No
Caller #3	Yes	No

🎧 12   LISTENING

Listen again to the conversations in Exercise 11. Compare your answers with your classmates. Did each applicant make a good impression? Why or why not?

GETTING INFORMATION FROM A MANAGER

After you tell the manager about your experience or transferable skills, the manager will tell you some information. This information can be the same information that a receptionist tells you.

- Come to the business and fill out an application.
- Send a resume.
- Come to the business for a job interview.
- There are no jobs. Call again.

After a manager tells you what to do, you need to get more information from him or her (for example, the name and the correct address of the company). Sometimes the manager will tell you this information, but sometimes you need to ask for this information.

🎧 13   LISTENING

You will hear five applicants calling about jobs and talking to managers. What does each caller need to do? Check (✔) the correct box.

	1	2	3	4	5
Go to the business and fill out an application.					
Send or fax a resume to the business.					
Go to the business for an interview.					
Call back in the future.					

HOW TO GET INFORMATION FROM A MANAGER

You *always* need to find out these things:

- The name of the company
- The manager's name

When the manager tells you to send a resume, you need to find out these things:

- The fax number

    or

- The address:
    — The number of the building
    — The name of the street (avenue, boulevard, road)
    — The location of the office in the building (room, suite, floor)
    — The ZIP code

When the manager tells you to come to a business and fill out an application, you need to find out these things:

- The street address
- The cross street or streets (the closest streets that go across the street the business is on)
- The business hours

When the manager tells you to come to the business for an interview, you need to find out these things:

- The street address
- The cross street or streets
- The day, date, and time of the interview

When the manager tells you to call back, you need to find this out:

- When to call back

14 WORDS FOR SUCCESS

Match the phrases on the left with the phrases on the right. Write the correct number on each line.

1. the street address	___ a.	94114
2. the ZIP code	___ b.	11:30 A.M.
3. the cross streets	_1_ c.	429 Grand Avenue
4. the day of the appointment	___ d.	Tuesday
5. the date of the appointment	___ e.	March 17th
6. the time of the appointment	___ f.	between 5th and 6th Streets

15 PAIR WORK

Work with a partner. Change the sentences to polite requests with *Could I, Could you,* or *May I.* Don't forget to use *please.*

1. What's the address?
2. Spell the name of the street.
3. What are the cross streets?

4. What's the ZIP code?
5. Repeat the number.
6. Spell the names of the cross streets.

LANGUAGE FOCUS
Saying and Understanding Addresses

When you talk to a manager, you often need the company's address. These examples will make it easier for you to say and understand addresses.

When the address has three numbers:

243 Main St.	You say, "Two, forty-three Main Street."
568 2nd Ave.	You say, "Five, sixty-eight Second Avenue."
700 23rd St.	You say, "Seven hundred Twenty-third Street."
605 Post Ave.	You say, "Six, oh, five Post Avenue."

When the address has four numbers:

1836 4th St.	You say, "Eighteen, thirty-six Fourth Street."
2855 18th Ave.	You say, "Twenty-eight, fifty-five Eighteenth Avenue."
9000 Taylor Rd.	You say, "Nine thousand Taylor Road."
7600 Grand Blvd.	You say, "Seventy-six hundred Grand Boulevard."
3009 41st St.	You say, "Three, oh, oh, nine Forty-first Street."

When the address has more than four numbers:

64579 Baker Ln.	You say, "Six, four, five, seven, nine Baker Lane."
10024 Oak Hill Rd.	You say, "One, oh, oh, two, four Oak Hill Road."

---

16 ON YOUR OWN

Write your address. Then write how you will say your address. (Look at the examples in the Language Focus box.)

Your address: _____

How you will say your address: _____

17 TEAM WORK

Work in small groups. Take turns asking for your classmates' addresses and telling them your address. Write your classmates' addresses. Ask questions when you don't understand.

1. _____

2. _____

3. _____

🎧 18 LISTENING

You will hear four applicants calling about jobs and talking to managers. Write down the information each applicant receives.

1. Street address: _____

   City and ZIP code: _____

   Manager's name: _____

2. Street address: _____

   Cross streets: _____

   Business hours: _____

   Manager's name: _____

3. Day of appointment: _____

   Date of appointment: _____

   Time of appointment: _____

   Street address: _____

   Cross streets: _____

4. Day of appointment: _____

   Date of appointment: _____

   Time of appointment: _____

   Street address: _____

   Cross streets: _____

LANGUAGE FOCUS
Checking Information

When you talk to a manager on the telephone, it is important to make sure that all the information you get is correct. You should always repeat the information you receive. Then you will know if the information is correct.

When the manager tells you names, addresses, days, dates, and times, always repeat the information to the manager. For example:

> Manager: The address is 111 Main Street.
> Applicant: 111 Main Street.

When you understand *part* of the information the manager tells you, repeat the part you understand. Then ask the manager to repeat the part you did not understand. For example:

> Manager: The address is 435 Delancy Street.
> Applicant: 435 . . . Could you repeat the street, please?

When you do *not* understand the information the manager tells you, ask the manager to repeat the information. For example:

> Manager: You can send your resume to Teri Burke.
> Applicant: Could you repeat the name, please?

19 PAIR WORK

INFORMATION GAP: Student A, look at this page. Student B, look at page 215.

1. Listen to your partner (Student B). Your partner will read some sentences. Write the important information (names, addresses, dates, and times) you hear. Repeat the information your partner tells you. Ask questions when you do not understand. Check the spelling of names and streets. When you finish, check your answers with your partner.

   a. _____

   b. _____

   c. _____

   d. _____

   e. _____

2. Talk to your partner (Student B). Read each sentence to your partner. Your partner will write down the important information you say. Answer your partner's questions. When you finish, check your partner's answers.

   f. My name is Kay Fang.

   g. The address is 2650 Margo Street, Suite 365.

   h. The ZIP code is 68147.

   i. The cross streets are Pearl and Sharp.

   j. Can you come in for an interview next Friday, May 18th, at 12:00?

⌒ 20 LISTENING

Listen to a telephone conversation between a job applicant and a manager. Fill in the blanks.

Manager: Could you come in for an interview next week?

Applicant: Yes, that's _____.

Manager: How about next Tuesday, June 14th, at 10:00?

Applicant: Excuse me. Could you _____ more _____, please?

Manager: Certainly. Next Tuesday, June 14th, at 10:00.

Applicant: Next Tuesday, June 14th, at 10:00?

Manager: Uh-huh.

Applicant: _____ _____. Could I have your address, please?

Manager: Sure. It's 4397 Oak Street, Suite 523.

Applicant: 4397 Oak Street. Could you _____ the _____ _____ , please?

Manager: Suite 523.

Applicant: Suite 523. I _____ . Could you tell me the _____ _____ , please?

Manager: We're between Park and Lakeshore.

Applicant: _____ . Between Park and Lakeshore?

Manager: Yes, that's right.

Applicant: And, could I have _____ _____ , please?

Manager: My name is Alicia Bolanos.

Applicant: Could you _____ your _____ name, please?

Manager: B–O–L /A–N as in Nancy /O–S.

Applicant: B–O–L /A–N/O–S?

Manager: Yes.

Applicant: Okay, Ms. Bolanos. I'll see you next Tuesday, June 14th, at 10:00. _____ _____ very much.

Manager: You're welcome. Goodbye.

Applicant: Goodbye.

21 PAIR WORK

Work with a partner. Practice the conversation in Exercise 20. When you finish, change roles.

22 PAIR WORK

Create a conversation with a partner. Student A is a manager and follows the directions on the left. Student B is a job applicant and follows the directions on the right. Applicants, ask polite questions when you do not understand. Remember to check your information. Applicants, be enthusiastic! When you finish, change roles.

MANAGER	APPLICANT
1. Introduce yourself.	1. Introduce yourself to the manager.
2. Say, "Can you tell me more about your experience?"	2. Tell the manager about your past job duties or more about your transferable skills.
3. Say, "Could you come in and fill out an application? We're open Monday through Friday from 9:00 to 5:00."	3. Ask for the address.
4. Say your address.	4. Repeat the address the manager told you, and write the address. Ask for cross streets.
5. Say your cross streets.	5. Repeat the cross streets the manager told you, and write the cross streets. Ask for the manager's name.
6. Say your name.	6. Repeat the name. Ask how to spell the manager's name.
7. Spell your name.	7. Repeat the spelling and write the manager's name. Say, "Thank you."
8. Say, "You're welcome. Goodbye."	8. Say, "Goodbye."

23 ROLE PLAYS

INFORMATION GAP: Student A, look at this page. Student B, look at page 216.

Work with a partner. Read the first situation. Then create a conversation. When you finish, read the second situation. Create another conversation.

1. Student A, you are a manager. Student B calls you about a job. Ask Student B to tell you more about his or her experience. Then make an appointment for an interview with him or her. Use this information:

   Interview appointment: Monday, April 22, 1:00 P.M.

   Manager's name: Cary Hakam

   Company address: 1361 Greenleaf Avenue, Suite 400

   Cross streets: Parker and Fell

2. Student A, you are a job applicant. You call Student B, a manager. Introduce yourself. Then tell the manager a little more about your experience or your transferable skills. Write the information the manager tells you. Repeat all of the information. Ask questions when you don't understand.

   Notes: _____

   _____

   _____

   _____

WHAT DO YOU THINK NOW?

Discuss these questions with your classmates.

1. When you are talking to a manager on the telephone, what should you say?
   What information should you tell a manager that you do not tell a receptionist?

2. What information should you get from a manager if he or she tells you to:

   • come in for an interview?
   • send a resume?
   • come in and fill out an application?

3. How can you make a good impression when you are talking on the telephone?

4. After you talk to a manager on the telephone, what will happen next?

24 REVIEW: Board Game

Listen to your teacher's instructions. Then play the game.

Spell the street. :(

Could I leave please a message ? ☆

She's not right in now. =

In my last job, I work at a hospital. ☆

What's her name ? :(

Could I make an appointment for an interview? =

Could I speak to the manager, please? =

I work as a _____. ☆
(Your past job title)

WINNER

I want an appointment for an interview. :(

I am call about the job as a bookkeeper. ☆

Why don't you send me your resume ? =

My telephone number 968-3594. ☆

My name is _____. =
(your name)

I see your job listing at the Career Center. ☆

I can drive a car. =

My friend Joan said me you have a job opening. ☆

Repeat, please. :)

I'm interesting in a job as a cashier. ☆

Tell me the cross streets. :)

Who should I say is calling ? =

START

I have two years' experience working in an office. =

Speak more slowly. :)

UNIT 5

Filling Out Job Applications: Personal Information and Position Desired

---

WHAT DO YOU THINK?

Discuss these questions with your classmates.

1. Did you ever fill out an application in your country (for example, an application to rent an apartment or an application to go to school)?
   What kind of application did you fill out?
   What kinds of applications have you filled out in this country?

2. When you apply for a job in your country, do you need to fill out a job application?
   If you do, what information do you need to write on job applications?

3. Did you ever fill out a job application here?
   If you did, what information did you write on the job application?

4. Why do managers want to look at job applications before they meet job applicants?
   What do managers think is important when they look at job applications?

In this unit, you will:

- Learn how to fill out job applications.

- Learn how to write information about yourself (personal information).

- Learn how to write information about the job you want (position desired).

- Learn what is important to managers when they look at job applications.

- Learn how you can make a good impression on your job applications.

AN INTRODUCTION TO JOB APPLICATIONS

When you apply for a job, you often fill out a job application before you have an interview with a manager. Managers want to see this information on job applications:

- Personal information: for example, your name, your address, and your telephone number
- Information about your past jobs, your skills, and your education

It is important to fill out a job application very carefully.

⌒ 1 LISTENING

You will hear three managers talking about how to fill out a job application. What is important to each manager? Write the number of the conversation next to the correct sentence.

__ Print or type your application.

__ Be neat and careful.

__ Answer *all* the questions.

Now turn to p. 216 and read the conversations that you just listened to. Check your answers.

2 WORDS FOR SUCCESS

Read the conversations on page 216 again. Then look at the underlined words in the following questions. What do the underlined words mean? Circle the correct letter.

1. When a job application is <u>complete</u>, you
   - (a.) answer all of the questions.
   - b. answer some of the questions.

2. When a manager <u>hires</u> a job applicant, he or she
   - a. gives the applicant an interview.
   - b. gives the applicant a job.

3. When you <u>follow instructions</u> on a job application, you
   - a. read the directions carefully and write the correct information.
   - b. ask a question when you do not understand.

4. An example of <u>handwriting</u> is
   - a. Mary Claycomb.
   - b. *Mary Claycomb.*

5. An example of <u>printing</u> is
   - a. Mary Claycomb.
   - b. *Mary Claycomb.*

6. When you do your work <u>neatly</u>, you work
   - a. very fast and don't worry about how your work looks.
   - b. very carefully and make sure your work looks nice.

(cont'd. on next page)

7. When you print <u>clearly</u>, your printing is
   a. difficult to read.
   b. easy to read.

8. When you <u>cross out</u> a word, you
   a. draw a line or an X through the word, for example:
      Geary ~~Blvd.~~ St.
   b. draw a circle around the word, for example:
      Geary (Blvd.) St.

9. When you make a <u>mistake</u>, you
   a. do something wrong.
   b. do something right.

10. When you <u>correct</u> an answer, you
    a. change a wrong answer to a right answer.
    b. give a right answer.

CULTURE NOTES

What Managers Look for on Job Applications

You need to fill out job applications very carefully because you want to make a good impression. Here are some ways to make a good impression.

Print or type your application:

- Check the alphabet on page 219 if you are not sure how to print a letter or letters.
- Use handwriting only when you *sign your name* (write your signature) at the end of the application (*James Cowan*).
- Use a pen, not a pencil.

Print your application neatly and clearly:

- Print slowly and carefully.
- Do not cross out words.
- If you make a mistake, ask for a new application, or use correction fluid and print the information again.

Complete your application:

- Follow the instructions carefully. Print the information in the correct spaces.
- Answer all of the questions about yourself, your experience, and your education.
- Print *N/A* (not applicable) in the correct space if you really *cannot answer* a question. For example, if you do not have a driver's license, you can write *N/A* on an application instead of a license number.

BE CAREFUL: Do *not* fill out all parts of some applications. For example, do *not* print information in these spaces:

FOR COMPANY USE ONLY
FOR OFFICE USE ONLY
DO NOT WRITE BELOW THIS LINE
DO NOT FILL OUT SPACE BELOW THIS LINE

3 ON YOUR OWN

You should print your answers on job applications. Practice your printing. If you are not sure of how to print a letter, look at page 219.

PART A

Change the handwriting to printing.

1. _technician_   technician _____

2. _Kano University_ _____

3. _725 Dalton Boulevard_ _____

4. _Pacific Center_ _____

5. _Rosario Chavez_ _____

PART B

Look at these words. Some letters are in handwriting. Some letters are in printing. Circle the letters in handwriting. Then print the words correctly.

1. Ti(g)ist Abe(n)(a)   Tigist Abena _____

2. _Kim Vuong_ _____

3. El Salvador _____

4. 87 Jefferson Ave. _____

5. _Beijing_ _____

4 PAIR WORK

Work with a partner. Margo and Paul filled out job applications. Look at part of their applications. Does Margo or Paul make a better impression? Why do you think so? How many mistakes can you find? Circle the mistakes.

MARGO'S APPLICATION

				TODAY'S DATE: 7/24/96

NAME:	Last Name Som	First Name Margo	Middle Name Anne	SOCIAL SECURITY NUMBER 124-38-7962

PRESENT HOME ADDRESS:	Street Number 521 Alvarado St.	City San Francisco	State CA	ZIP Code 94114

HOME PHONE: (415) 282-3469	WORK PHONE: N/A

YES ☐ NO ☑ Are you under 21 years of age?	POSITION DESIRED: Sales Clerk

HOURS THAT YOU ARE AVAILABLE TO WORK ON EACH OF THESE DAYS:

	SUNDAY	MONDAY	TUESDAY	WEDNESDAY	THURSDAY	FRIDAY	SATURDAY
From:	9:00 a.m.						
To:	10:00 p.m.						

FOR COMPANY USE ONLY:

STARTING DATE 8/96	SALARY $6/hour	POSITION Sales

HIRED BY N/A ?	COMPANY LOCATION San Francisco, CA

PAUL'S APPLICATION

				TODAY'S DATE: 24/7/96

NAME:	Last Name Paul	First Name Kaganov	Middle Name S.	SOCIAL SECURITY NUMBER — —

PRESENT HOME ADDRESS:	Street Number Townsend Ave. 123	City S.F.	State Ca	ZIP Code 94137 57

HOME PHONE: (415) 641-03-44	WORK PHONE:

YES ☐ NO ☐ Are you under 21 years of age?	POSITION DESIRED: S ƒales clerk

HOURS THAT YOU ARE AVAILABLE TO WORK ON EACH OF THESE DAYS:

	SUNDAY	MONDAY	TUESDAY	WEDNESDAY	THURSDAY	FRIDAY	SATURDAY
From:	8:00 a.m.	8:00 a.m.	8:00 a.m.	8:00 a.m.	8:00 a.m.	8:00 a.m.	8:00 a.m.
To:	6:00 p.m.	6:00 p.m.	6:00 p.m.	6:00 p.m.	6:00 p.m.	6:00 p.m.	6:00 p.m.

FOR COMPANY USE ONLY:

STARTING DATE	SALARY	POSITION

HIRED BY	COMPANY LOCATION

Personal Information

At the beginning of a job application, you need to fill out the date of the application and some basic **personal information** (information about yourself). The person who does the hiring needs this information so that he or she can contact (call or write) you.

HOW TO FILL OUT INFORMATION ABOUT YOURSELF

You need to fill out this information about yourself:

- **The date:** Write the month first. Then write the day and the year. Write the date like this: month / day / year.

- **Your name:** On most applications, you should write your last name (family name) first. Then write your first name (given name) and your middle name or middle initial (M.I.).

- **Your present address:** This is where you are living now. Write your address in this order: the street number, the street name (and the apartment number), the city, the state, and the ZIP code.

- **Permanent address:** This is the place where you will live for a long time. If you will live at your present address for a long time, you can write *Same* for your permanent address.

- **Your home telephone number:** Write your area code and telephone number.

- **Your business telephone number:** If you are working now, write the area code and phone number of your workplace. If you are not working, print *N/A*.

- **Your social security number:** Write your social security number. Use dashes, like this: 000-00-0000.

5 PAIR WORK

Stewart filled out two job applications correctly. Here is one part of each application. On each application he filled in the same information, but some of the words on the applications are different.

Look at the applications with a partner. How many differences can you find? Match the words with the same meaning. Write the correct number in each circle. Then discuss the questions that follow the applications.

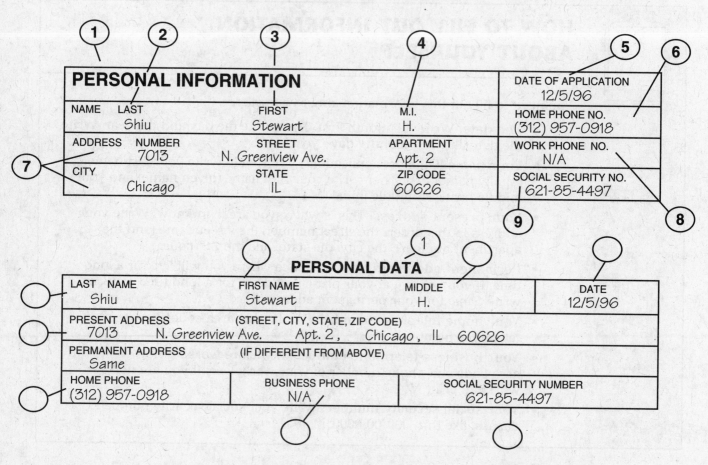

1. Look at the date (12/5/96). What are the month, day, and year?

2. Look at Stewart's name. Did he print his first name or his last name first?

3. Do you write your first name or your last name first in your country? In this country?

4. Do you say your first name or last name first in your country? In this country?

6 WORDS FOR SUCCESS

Look again at Stewart's job applications in Exercise 5. Circle the correct letter to complete each sentence.

1. The applicant's name is
   a. Shiu H. Stewart.
   b. Stewart H. Shiu.

2. The applicant's middle initial is
   a. H.
   b. S.

3. The applicant filled out this application form on
   a. May 12.
   b. December 5.

4. The applicant lives in
   a. a house.
   b. an apartment.

5. The applicant's area code is
   a. 60626.
   b. 312.

6. The applicant's ZIP code is
   a. 60626.
   b. 312.

7. The applicant's present address and permanent address are
   a. the same.
   b. different.

8. The applicant's street address is
   a. Chicago, IL 60626.
   b. 7013 N. Greenview Ave., Apt 2.

9. The applicant's state is
   a. IL (Illinois).
   b. Chicago.

10. The applicant _____ a business telephone.
    a. has
    b. doesn't have

LANGUAGE FOCUS

Capitalization and Punctuation

When you fill out a job application, it is important to know about capitalization. When do you need to print a capital letter (A, B, C)? When do you need to print a small letter (a, b, c)?

It is also important to know about punctuation. How do you use slashes (/), dashes (-), commas (,) and periods (.)?

---

7 PAIR WORK

Look again at Stewart's job applications in Exercise 5. Then discuss these questions with a partner.

1. When did Stewart use capital letters? When did he use small letters?

2. Where did Stewart put slashes (/), dashes (-), commas (,), and periods (.)?

8 PAIR WORK

Now look at Adinah's application. Correct her mistakes on your own. Circle the letters that Adinah does not print correctly. Put slashes (/), dashes (-), commas (,), and periods (.) in the correct places. Then compare your answers with your partner's answers.

PERSONAL INFORMATION				DATE 9. 13. 95	
NAME bARnEtt AdinAh f				SOCIAL SECURITY NUMBER 128-3760-42	
LAST FIRST MIDDLE					
PRESENT ADDRESS 103 gRAnt st Apt 2 poRtlAnd mE 04101					
STREET CITY STATE ZIP					
PERMANENT ADDRESS sAmE					
STREET CITY STATE ZIP					
HOME PHONE (207) 761-18-19 WORK PHONE n/A					

9 ON YOUR OWN

Here is the first part of a job application. Fill out information about yourself.

APPLICATION FOR EMPLOYMENT

PERSONAL INFORMATION	Date	Social Security Number		
Name				
Present Address	Last First Middle			
Permanent Address	Street	City	State	ZIP
Home Phone No.	Street	City Business Phone No.	State	ZIP

10 ON YOUR OWN

On some job applications, you need to print information in a *very* small space. Copy the information you filled out in Exercise 9. Be sure that your printing is small.

APPLICATION FOR EMPLOYMENT

PERSONAL INFORMATION	Date	Social Security Number		
Name				
Present Address	Last First Middle			
Permanent Address	Street	City	State	ZIP
Home Phone No.	Street	City Business Phone No.	State	ZIP

HOW TO FILL OUT YOUR EMERGENCY CONTACT INFORMATION
Who Should the Manager Call?

If you become very sick or if you have an accident when you are working, your manager needs to know how to notify (call) a person who can help you.

On a job application, you need to fill out the name, address, and telephone number of a *good friend* or a *person in your family*. Who should your manager call if you become sick or have an accident at work?

11   ON YOUR OWN

Fill out information about your emergency contact. Print the name, address, and telephone number of a family member or a good friend.

IN CASE OF EMERGENCY, PLEASE NOTIFY

Name _____   Home Address _____   Home Phone (_____) _____-_____

Work Address _____   Work Phone (_____) _____-_____

HOW TO FILL OUT MORE INFORMATION ABOUT YOURSELF

On some job applications, you need to fill out other information about yourself:

- **Your job now:** Are you working now? Can the person who does the hiring call your manager? Answer *Yes* or *No*. If you are working, you sometimes need to write your manager's name.

- **Your relationship to the company:** Have you ever applied to this company before? Do any of your relatives work at this company? Answer *Yes* or *No*. If any of your relatives work in the company, write their names.

- **Other names you have used:** Have you ever used another name? Write other names you had in the past. For example, if you had a different name before you got married, write that name. If you did not have any other names, write *N/A*.

- **Your age:** Are you eighteen years of age or older? Answer *Yes* or *No*. If you are under eighteen, you sometimes need to show proof of your age (for example, a driver's license, an identification (I.D.) card, a work permit). Answer *Yes* or *No* after questions about proof of age and work permit. If you are eighteen or older, write *N/A* after questions about proof of age.

- **Your legal right to work:** Are you a U.S. citizen? Answer *Yes* or *No*. If you are not a U.S. citizen, do you have the legal right to work in the United States? Answer *Yes* or *No*. All people must be able to show that they have the legal right to work in the United States before they can begin to work. Managers need to see your legal papers that show you can work (for example, a social security card, work authorization on a passport, a green card).

12 PAIR WORK

Stewart filled out two job applications correctly. Here is one part of each application. On each application, he filled in the same information, but some of the words on the applications are different. Look at the applications with a partner. How many differences can you find? Match the words that have the same meaning. Write the correct number in each circle.

(1) Are you 18 years of age or older?   Yes ☑   No ☐   **(2)** If not, can you submit a work permit?   Yes ☐   No ☐   N/A

Are you a U.S. citizen?   Yes ☐   No ☑   Are you authorized to work in the U.S.?   Yes ☑   No ☐   **(3)**

(4) Are you working now?   Yes ☑   No ☐   If so, may we inquire of your present supervisor?   Yes ☑   No ☐   **(5)**

If so, where?   Fortuna Bakery

Employer's name   Sophia Chang

(6) List other last names used   N/A

(7) Do you have any relatives presently employed by us?   Yes ☐   No ☑

Have you ever applied to this company before?   Yes ☐   No ☑   **(8)**

(9) Have you ever worked for this company before?   Yes ☐   No ☑

Are you a U.S. citizen?   Yes ☐   No ☑   If not, are you legally eligible to work?   Yes ☑   No ☐   ◯

(1) Are you 18 or over?   Yes ☑   No ☐   If you are under 18, can you provide a work permit?   Yes ☐   No ☐   N/A   ◯

◯ Have you filled out an application here before?   ☐ Yes   ☑ No

◯ Are you related to anyone in this company?   ☐ Yes   ☑ No

◯ Have you previously been employed by this company?   ☐ Yes   ☑ No   ◯

◯ Are you employed now?   Yes ☑   No ☐   May we contact your present employer?   Yes ☑   No ☐

◯ Have you ever used another name?   Yes ☐   No ☑   If yes, give other names used.   N/A

13 ON YOUR OWN

Here are some questions you might find on job applications. Write the different ways to ask the same questions, using the questions in the box.

PART A

> Have you ever worked or attended school under another name?
> May we contact your employer?
> ✔ Are you employed now?
> Are you currently employed?
> May we inquire of your present employer?
> Other last names used?

1. Are you working now?

   Are you employed now?
   _____

2. Can we speak to your current supervisor?

   _____

   _____

3. Have you ever used another name?

   _____

   _____

PART B

> Do you have any relatives presently employed by us?
> Have you ever worked for this company before?
> Are you related to anyone in our company?
> Have you ever filed an application with this company before?
> Have you previously been employed by this company?
> Have you ever applied to this company before?

4. Did you fill out an application here before?

   _____

   _____

5. Did you work here before?

   _____

   _____

6. Do your relatives work here?

   _____

   _____

14 WORDS FOR SUCCESS

Circle the correct letter to complete each sentence.

1. This employer will only hire workers who are eighteen years old or more than eighteen years old. You must be

   a. at least eighteen years old.
   b. under eighteen years old.

2. If you are not eighteen years old or over, you sometimes need to show the manager identification (I.D.) that shows your age. You must show the manager

   a. other names you have used.
   b. proof of age.

3. If the government says that you are eligible to work (you can work) in the United States, you have the legal right to work in the United States. You are

   a. authorized to work.
   b. prevented from working.

4. If the government says that you are *not* eligible to work (you *cannot* work) in the United States, you do *not* have the legal right to work in the United States. You are

   a. authorized to work.
   b. prevented from working.

5. You must show the manager your legal papers before you can start to work in the United States. You must submit (show) the manager verification of

   a. your age.
   b. your right to work.

15   PAIR WORK

You are helping some people fill out job applications. Read each story with a partner. Fill out the application after each story.

1. Alex is seventeen years old. He moved to the United States with his family three months ago. He has a legal right to work in the United States.

Are you a U.S. citizen?   ☐ Yes   ☑ No

Are you legally eligible for employment in the U.S.?   ☑ Yes   ☐ No

Are you at least 18 years of age?   ☐ Yes   ☑ No

---

2. Clarissa is twenty-five years old, and she came to the United States three years ago. She has a green card now, and she is looking for a job as a driver. She is very happy because she just got an Illinois driver's license.

Are you a U.S. citizen?   Yes _____ No _____   **If hired, can you furnish proof of age ?**   Yes _____ No _____

Are you legally authorized or permitted to work in the United States?   Yes _____ No _____   **If you are under 18 years old, can you submit a work permit?**   Yes _____ No _____

(cont'd. on next page)

3. Shari lives in San Francisco, California, and wants to work for Werner's, a large clothing company. She worked for the same company in El Paso, Texas, in 1995. She is the only one in her family who works for Werner's, and she does not know anyone at the company in California.

Have you ever been employed by Werner's? Yes _____	No _____
If so, where? _____	When? _____
Are any of your relatives employed by Werner's? Yes _____	No _____
Name _____	Relationship _____
Location _____	

4. Nicolas is working now, but he wants a new job. His aunt, Rene Vasquez, works for Pacific Services and told Nicolas that there is a good opening at Pacific Services now. He is applying to Pacific Services for the first time. Nicolas told his manager, Doug, that he is looking for a new job, so a manager at Pacific Services can call Doug.

Are you currently employed? ☐ Yes ☐ No   May we contact your employer? ☐ Yes ☐ No

Have you ever applied to Pacific Services before? ☐ Yes ☐ No

Where? _____   When? _____

Name and relationship of any relatives in this company _____

16 ON YOUR OWN

Here is part of a job application. Fill out information about yourself.

Are you currently employed? ☐ Yes ☐ No	If yes, can we speak to your present supervisor? ☐ Yes ☐ No
Have you ever worked or attended school under a different name? ☐ Yes ☐ No	If yes, give other name(s) used:
Are you 18 years of age or older? ☐ Yes ☐ No	If under 18, can you submit a work permit? ☐ Yes ☐ No

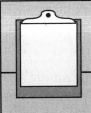

HOW TO FILL OUT INFORMATION ABOUT YOUR CRIMINAL RECORD

On some job applications, you need to fill out information about your **criminal record** (problems with the police or with the law). Here are some words that mean "crime": *felony, violation, offense.* There are usually two questions about your criminal record.

The first question asks if you ever had problems with the police or the law.

- Answer *Yes* or *No.*

The second question asks you to give information about your criminal record if you answered *Yes* to the first question.

- If you never had problems with the police or the law, answer *No.* Print *N/A* to answer the question, *"If yes, . . ."*

- If you had problems with the police or the law, ask someone to help you answer this question.

17 PAIR WORK

Stewart filled out two job applications correctly. Here is part of each application. On each application, he filled in the same information, but some of the words on the application are different. Look at the applications with a partner. How many differences can you find? Match the words that have the same meaning. Write the correct number in each circle.

(1) **HAVE YOU EVER BEEN CONVICTED OF A FELONY?**

☐ YES   ☑ NO

(2) **IF YES, EXPLAIN EACH OCCURRENCE AND GIVE DATES.**

N/A

( ) **HAVE YOU EVER BEEN CONVICTED OF A CRIMINAL VIOLATION?**   YES ____   NO ✔

( ) **IF YES, EXPLAIN.** ____ N/A _____

POSITION DESIRED

On job applications, you need to fill out information about the position desired (the job you want). The person who does the hiring needs to know the name of the job you are applying for, the hours and days that you can work, and the salary you want.

HOW TO FILL OUT INFORMATION ABOUT THE JOB YOU WANT

You need to fill out this information about the job you want:

- **The job title:** Write the name of the job you want.

- **The date available:** Write the date that you can start to work. If you can start to work right away, write *Immediately*.

- **The schedule you can work:** Managers want to know when you can work. For example: Can you work in the evenings? Can you work on the weekends? You may find different words that mean "schedule" on job applications:

  — Days and hours: Write the days and times you can work.
  — Shift desired: In some companies, there are three shifts:

    Day (7:00 A.M.–3:30 P.M.)
    Swing or Evening (3:00 P.M.–11:30 P.M.)
    Night (11:00 P.M.–7:30 A.M.)
    Indicate the shift you prefer.

- **Type of employment desired:** Managers want to know how many hours you can work a week:

    Full-time (usually 35–40 hours a week)
    Part-time (usually less than 35 hours a week)

  Managers are also interested in how long you want to work:

    Permanent (for a long time)
    Temporary (for a short time)

  Indicate the type of employment you prefer.

- **Salary desired:** Managers are interested in the salary you would like. When you see a question about salary on a job application, you can write *Open*. This means you are flexible about salary. We will discuss this more in Unit 7.

18 PAIR WORK

Stewart filled out two job applications correctly. Here is one part of each application. On each application, he filled in the same information, but some of the words on the applications are different. Look at the applications with a partner. How many differences can you find? Match the words that have the same meaning. Write the correct number in each circle.

(1)

POSITION OBJECTIVE

POSITION DESIRED		DATE AVAILABLE TO WORK **(2)**
Certified Nurse's Assistant		Immediately

SHIFT DESIRED	TYPE OF EMPLOYMENT DESIRED **(3)**
☑ Day ☑ Swing ☐ Night ☐ Other	☑ Full-Time ☑ Part-Time ☑ Permanent ☐ Temporary

(5)

SALARY / WAGE DESIRED **(4)**	PLEASE SPECIFY DAYS AND HOURS AVAILABLE
Open	☑ Mon 7:00 A.M.–11:00 P.M. ☑ Tues 7:00 A.M.–11:00 P.M. ☑ Wed 7:00 A.M.–11:00 P.M. ☑ Thurs 7:00 A.M.–11:00 P.M. ☑ Fri 7:00 A.M.–11:00 P.M. ☑ Sat 7:00 A.M.–11:00 P.M. ☑ Sun 7:00 A.M.–11:00 P.M.

(1)

EMPLOYMENT DESIRED

POSITION APPLYING FOR _____ Certified Nurse's Assistant _____   DATE YOU CAN START _Immediately_

( ) Please check ____ Full-Time ☑ Part-Time ☑ Permanent ☑ Temporary ☐

( ) Please specify DAYS and HOURS

DAY	SUNDAY	MONDAY	TUESDAY	WEDNESDAY	THURSDAY	FRIDAY	SATURDAY
FROM	7:00 A.M.	7:00 A.M.	7:00 A.M.	7:00 A.M.	7:00 A.M.	7:00 A.M.	7:00 A.M.
TO	11:00 P.M.	11:00 P.M.	11:00 P.M.	11:00 P.M.	11:00 P.M.	11:00 P.M.	11:00 P.M.

( ) MINIMUM SALARY DESIRED _____ Open _____

19 WORDS FOR SUCCESS

Complete the sentences, using the words or phrases in the boxes.

PART A

part-time	night	evening	swing
shift	full-time	✔position applying for	

1. The name of the job you want is called type of work desired, position
    objective, or _____position applying for_____.

2. A _____ is your work schedule: day, swing,
    evening, or night.

3. If you work from 7:00 A.M. to 4:00 P.M., you work the day shift.
    If you work from 3:00 P.M. to 12:00 A.M., you work the _____
    or the _____ shift. If you work from 11:00 P.M. to 8:00 A.M., you
    work the _____ shift.

4. If you work all day long, five days a week, you work _____.
    If you work only a few hours each day or a few days each week, you
    work _____.

PART B

minimum salary	preferred	temporary	open
immediately	salary desired	date available	

5. Shift preference or _____ shift means the work
    hours that are best for you.

6. If you have a permanent job, your job will not end soon. If you have a
    _____ job, your job will end in a short time.

7. The date you can start your new job is the _____.
    If you can start to work now, you should write _____.

8. The salary you want is the _____. The lowest salary
    you will accept is the _____.

9. When you have an interview with the manager, you can talk about
    the salary. When you read *Salary* on job applications, you can
    write _____.

20 ON YOUR OWN

Here is the Position Desired part of a job application. Fill out information about yourself.

POSITION DESIRED							
MINIMUM SALARY DESIRED				DATE AVAILABLE FOR WORK			
TYPE OF EMPLOYMENT DESIRED							
FULL-TIME ☐		PART-TIME ☐		TEMPORARY ☐		PERMANENT ☐	
DAYS AND HOURS YOU ARE AVAILABLE TO WORK:							
Hours	SUN	MON	TUES	WED	THURS	FRI	SAT
From							
To							

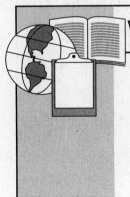

WHAT DO YOU THINK NOW?

Discuss these questions with your classmates.

1. What is some information you need to fill out on job applications in this country?

2. Why do managers want to look at job applications before they meet job applicants?
   What do managers think is important when they look at job applications?

21 REVIEW: Game

Listen to your teacher's instructions. Then play the game.

PART-TIME	OTHER LAST NAMES USED	20 HOURS PER WEEK	ARE YOU 18 YEARS OF AGE OR OVER ?	DID YOU WORK HERE BEFORE ?
NIGHT SHIFT	ARE YOU LESS THAN 18 YEARS OLD ?	EMPLOYMENT DESIRED	NOT PERMANENT	CAN WE INQUIRE OF YOUR PRESENT EMPLOYER ?
BUSINESS PHONE	HAVE YOU PREVIOUSLY BEEN EMPLOYED BY THIS COMPANY?	ARE YOU CURRENTLY EMPLOYED ?	M.I.	ARE YOU AUTHORIZED TO WORK ?
POSITION APPLYING FOR	WAGE DESIRED	HAVE YOU EVER WORKED OR ATTENDED SCHOOL UNDER A DIFFERENT NAME?	DATE AVAILABLE	TEMPORARY
ARE YOU LEGALLY ELIGIBLE TO WORK ?	ARE YOU OVER 18 ?	SCHEDULE: 11:00 P.M.– 7:30 A.M.	WORK PHONE	SALARY DESIRED
ARE YOU WORKING NOW ?	MIDDLE INITIAL	CAN WE SPEAK TO YOUR CURRENT SUPERVISOR ?	ARE YOU UNDER 18 YEARS OLD ?	DATE YOU CAN START

UNIT 6

Filling Out Job Applications: Work History, Education, and References

WHAT DO YOU THINK?

Discuss these questions with your classmates.

1. What do you know about the educational system in this country?
   Is the educational system the same or different in your country?

2. Do managers ask you for references (people who know you and can tell a manager about you) in your country?
   What information do managers want to find out from references?

3. Did you need a resume in your country?
   If you did, what information did you need to write on your resume?
   If you did not have a resume, did you have another kind of document?
   What information do you need to write on a resume in this country?

4. What information do you need to write in a cover letter (a letter you send with a resume to introduce yourself to a manager)?

In this unit, you will:

- Learn how to fill out information about your work history (your past jobs).

- Learn how to fill out information about your education.

- Learn how to fill out information about your references.

- Learn how to write a resume.

- Learn how to write a cover letter.

Work history

On most job applications, you need to fill out information about your past jobs. The manager wants to know where you worked, how long you worked, and what kind of work you did.

When you fill out information about your work history, you need to list your most recent job (last job) first. If you are working now, you should list your current job first because it is your most recent job. You should also list your volunteer work (work that is not paid).

HOW TO FILL OUT INFORMATION ABOUT YOUR WORK HISTORY

You need to fill out this information about your work history:

- **The name and address of your past company / employer:**

BE CAREFUL: Do *not* write your supervisor's name when you read "Employer." Write the name and the address of the company.

- **Your supervisor's name:** Who told you what to do at work? Write the first name and the last name of this person.

- **The telephone number of your company or your supervisor:** Write the area code and telephone number of your past company or your supervisor.

- **The dates you worked:** When you read "From," write the date (month/year) you *started* your job. When you read "To," write the date (month/year) you *finished* your job.

- **Your job title:** Write the name of your past job.

- **Your job duties:** Write three or more of your job duties. Use the past tense for your past job duties. Use the present tense for your current job duties.

- **Your salary:** When you read "Starting salary," write the first salary you received. When you read "Final salary," write the last salary you received. If you worked in another country, you can write *N/A*.

- **Your reason for leaving:** Managers want to know why you left your last job. Write the reason you left your job. Here are some reasons for leaving:

emigrated	=	I left my home country.
moved	=	I went to another city to live.
better opportunity	=	I found a job with a better salary, *or*
		I found a job that I liked more than my old job.
promotion	=	I got a better job in the same company.
career change	=	I found a different kind of job.

1 PAIR WORK

Anna filled out two job applications correctly. Here is one part of each application. On each application, she filled in the same information, but some of the words on the applications are different. Look at the applications with a partner. How many differences can you find? Match the words that have the same meaning. Write the correct number in each circle.

EMPLOYMENT BACKGROUND

List present or most recent employment first

1. Employer	Start Date Mo./Yr.	End Date Mo./Yr.	Job Title and Duties	
Eldercare Action			Home Health Aide	
Street Address	1/94	present	Help elderly patient: dress, cook, bathe	
1209 O'Farrell St.				
City, State, ZIP Code	Last Supervisor's Name		Telephone Number	Start Salary
San Francisco, CA 94108	Ruth Cowan		(415) 954-3372	$8.00/ hr
Reason for Leaving				Last Salary
N/A				$10.00/ hr
2. Employer	Start Date Mo./Yr.	End Date Mo./Yr.	Job Title and Duties	
Department of Culture			Accountant: Paid company's bills, paid employees' salaries, prepared information about the company's income	
Street Address	3/83	10/93		
15 Ukraine Blvd.				
City, State, Zip Code	Last Supervisor's Name		Telephone Number	Start Salary
Kiev, Ukraine	Ludmila Ivanova		164-6288	$ N/A
Reason for Leaving				Last Salary
Emigrated				$ N/A

WORK EXPERIENCE

Begin with the most current employer

COMPANY	Eldercare Action	PHONE NUMBER (415) 954-3372	
ADDRESS STREET CITY STATE ZIP	1209 O'Farrell St. San Francisco CA 94108	EMPLOYMENT DATES FROM: 1/94 TO: present	
POSITION HELD	Home Health Aide	STARTING SALARY $8.00/hr	PRESENT/FINAL SALARY $10.00/hr
DESCRIPTION OF YOUR WORK	Help elderly patient: dress, cook, bathe		
IMMEDIATE SUPERVISOR	Ruth Cowan	REASON FOR LEAVING N/A	
COMPANY	Department of Culture	PHONE NUMBER 164-6288	
ADDRESS STREET CITY STATE ZIP	15 Ukraine Blvd. Kiev Ukraine —	EMPLOYMENT DATES FROM: 3/83 TO: 10/93	
POSITION HELD	Accountant	STARTING SALARY N/A	PRESENT/FINAL SALARY N/A
DESCRIPTION OF YOUR WORK	Paid company's bills, paid employees' salaries, prepared information about company's income		
IMMEDIATE SUPERVISOR	Ludmila Ivanova	REASON FOR LEAVING Emigrated	

2 WORDS FOR SUCCESS

Look again at Anna's job applications in Exercise 1. Circle the correct letter to complete each sentence.

1. The street address of Anna's most recent job is
   a. 1209 O'Farrell Street.
   b. 15 Ukraine Boulevard.

2. Anna's job duties at her present job are
   a. a home health aide.
   b. to help elderly patient: dress, cook, bathe.

3. Anna's job title at the Department of Culture was
   a. Accountant.
   b. Paid company's bills, paid employees' salaries.

4. Anna's employer in 1984 was
   a. Ludmila Ivanova.
   b. the Department of Culture.

5. Anna's present supervisor is
   a. Ruth Cowan.
   b. Eldercare Action.

6. Anna's salary now is
   a. $8.00 per hour.
   b. $10.00 per hour.

3 ON YOUR OWN

Here is the Work History part of a job application. Fill out information about yourself.

EMPLOYMENT HISTORY List PRESENT or LAST employer first

FROM		TO		EMPLOYER'S NAME AND COMPLETE ADDRESS (COMPANY NAME, STREET NO., CITY, STATE AND ZIP CODE)		
MO	YR	MO	YR			
STARTING SALARY		ENDING SALARY		YOUR JOB TITLE:	IMMEDIATE SUPERVISOR:	TELEPHONE
$ PER		$ PER				( )
DESCRIPTION OF DUTIES:						
REASON FOR LEAVING:						
FROM		TO		EMPLOYER'S NAME AND COMPLETE ADDRESS (COMPANY NAME, STREET NO., CITY, STATE AND ZIP CODE)		
MO	YR	MO	YR			
STARTING SALARY		ENDING SALARY		YOUR JOB TITLE:	IMMEDIATE SUPERVISOR:	TELEPHONE
$ PER		$ PER				( )
DESCRIPTION OF DUTIES:						
REASON FOR LEAVING:						

EDUCATION

On most job applications, you need to fill out information about your education. You need to understand the system of education in the United States to fill out this part of a job application. All schools in the United States are not the same, but you can use the following information to fill out job applications.

4 ON YOUR OWN

Read about education in the United States. Then fill in the chart that follows.

EDUCATION IN THE UNITED STATES: ELEMENTARY SCHOOL, MIDDLE SCHOOL, AND HIGH SCHOOL

Most children go to **elementary school** (grammar school) for seven years. They are in **kindergarten** for the first year of elementary school. For the next six years, they are in **grades**, or levels: first grade, second grade, third grade, fourth grade, fifth grade, and sixth grade.

After sixth grade, most students change schools and begin **middle school** (junior high school). They usually attend middle school for two years: seventh grade and eighth grade.

When students finish middle school, they go to **high school**. Students usually attend high school for four years: ninth grade, tenth grade, eleventh grade, and twelfth grade.

When students finish or **graduate** from high school, they receive a **high school diploma** (a special document). If students do not finish high school, they can take a test called the Graduate Equivalency Diploma exam (G.E.D.). If they pass the test, they get a G.E.D. This is similar to a high school diploma.

School	Number of Years	Grades	Diploma
Grammar school		Kindergarten Grades 1–6	None
	2 years		None
High school		Grades 9–12	

5 ON YOUR OWN

Read more about education in the United States. Then fill in the chart that follows on page 131.

EDUCATION IN THE UNITED STATES: AFTER HIGH SCHOOL

After high school, some students go to **vocational school** (trade school, technical school, or business school) to learn a skill that they can use in a job; for example, refrigeration repair. Students usually attend vocational school from six months to two years. If students study for less than two years, they usually receive a **certificate**. If students graduate after two years, they usually receive an **associate's degree**. Students can receive an **Associate of Arts degree (A.A.)** or an **Associate of Science degree (A.S.)**.

Some students go to **two-year colleges** after they graduate from high school; for example, community college. Other students go to **four-year colleges** or **universities** after they graduate from high school. Some students continue on and study at a **four-year college** or at a **university** after they graduate from a two-year college.

In colleges and universities, each student chooses his or her most important subject. This subject is called a **major**. For example, Marc wants to become a teacher, so he is studying education. Education is his major. Consuela wants to be an electrical engineer, so she is studying electrical engineering. Electrical engineering is her major.

When students graduate after two years of college, they receive an **associate's degree** (A.A. or A.S.).

When students graduate after four years of college or university, they receive a **bachelor's degree**. Most students receive a **Bachelor of Arts degree (B.A.)**, or a **Bachelor of Science degree (B.S.)**. For example, Marc is studying education. When he graduates, he will receive a Bachelor of Arts degree (B.A.). Consuela is studying electrical engineering. When she graduates, she will receive a Bachelor of Science degree (B.S.).

Some students continue to study in **graduate school** after they receive a bachelor's degree. When students finish the first level of graduate school, they receive a **master's degree**. Most students receive a **Master of Arts degree (M.A.)** or a **Master of Science degree (M.S.)**. After students receive a master's degree, they can study for a **doctorate degree (Ph.D.)**. A doctorate degree is the highest level of education in the United States.

School	Number of years	Degree or certificate
Vocational school	6 months–2 years	
	2 years	Associate of Arts (A.A.) Associate of Science (A.S.)
College/University	4 years	
	1 or more years	Master of Arts (M.A.) Master of Science (M.S.) Doctorate (Ph.D.)

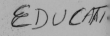

HOW TO FILL OUT INFORMATION ABOUT YOUR EDUCATION

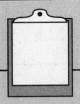

You need to fill out this information about your education on a job application:

- **The name and address of your school:** Write the name of each school. If your school had a number, write the number and the school; for example, Odessa School #15. Then write the address. On most applications, you need to write the city and the state (or the country).
- **How long you went to the school:** Sometimes you need to write the number of years you attended a school. Sometimes you need to write the dates you attended a school.
  - **Years completed:** Write a number; for example, 4.
  - **Dates attended:** Sometimes you need to write the dates you attended a college or university. Write the month and the year you started. Then write the month and the year you graduated.
- **If you graduated from the school:** Answer *Yes* or *No*.
- **What you studied at the school:** If you studied many different subjects (in elementary school or high school), write *General*. If you had a major (in college or graduate school), write your major.
- **What type of diploma or degree you received:** Write *Diploma* if you graduated from high school. If you graduated from a technical school or from a college or university, write the type of degree or certificate you received.

EDUCATI

FINAL

6 PAIR WORK

Rosa filled out two job applications correctly. Here is one part of each application. On each application, she filled in the same information, but some of the words on the applications are different. Look at the applications with a partner. How many differences can you find? Match the words that have the same meaning. Write the correct number in each circle.

① ②   ③ ④   ⑤ ⑥

EDUCATION AND TRAINING

SCHOOL	NAME AND ADDRESS	NUMBER OF YEARS COMPLETED	GRADUATED		MAJOR	DEGREE
⑦ HIGH SCHOOL	Technical High School #27 Jalisco, Mexico	4	Ⓨ	N	General	Diploma
⑧ COLLEGE/ UNIVERSITY	University of Mexico, Mexico City, Mexico	4	Ⓨ	N	Accounting	B.S.
⑨ ADDITIONAL TRAINING			Y	N		

①

EDUCATION

SCHOOL	NAME AND LOCATION OF SCHOOL	Dates attended		Course of study	Circle last year completed				Did you graduate?	List diploma or degree
High	Technical High School #27 Jalisco, Mexico	✕		General	1	2	3	④	☒ Yes ☐ No	Diploma
College	University of Mexico Mexico City, Mexico	From 9/78	To 6/82	Accounting	1	2	3	④	☒ Yes ☐ No	B.S.
Trade, Business, or Vocational School		From	To		1	2	3	4		

7 WORDS FOR SUCCESS

Complete the sentences, using the words in the boxes.

PART A

degree	vocational school	grades	major
✔ diploma	kindergarten	middle school	

1. When students graduate from high school, they receive a(n) _diploma_.

2. In elementary school, children go to _kindergarten_ and six _grades_.

3. When students graduate from college or university, they receive a(n) _degree_.

4. Students attend _middle school_ after they attend elementary school.

5. Karl is studying biology at the University of Texas because he wants to be a biology teacher. Biology is his _major_.

6. Elaine studied cosmetology at Miss Marty's School of Beauty for six months. Miss Marty's is a(n) _vocational school_.

PART B

Master of Science degree	Ph.D.
Bachelor of Science degree	Associate of Arts degree
Master of Arts degree	certificate

7. A doctoral degree is also called a(n) _Ph.D_.

8. If you study history, literature, or language for two years, you receive a(n) _A.A._ when you graduate.

9. When you finish the first level of graduate school, you can receive a(n) _master of_ or a(n) _m.a_.

10. If you finish a six-month course at vocational school, you can receive a(n) _certificate_.

11. If you study mathematics, engineering, or biology for four years in college, you receive a(n) _B.S_ when you graduate.

8 PAIR WORK

Work with a partner. Read each story. Then fill out each application based on the information in the story.

1. Yodit went to Adiugri High School in Adiugri, Eritrea, for four years. She graduated in 1984 and received a high school diploma. After high school, she studied education at the Asmara University in Asmara, Eritrea, for four years and received a Bachelor of Arts degree. When she came to the United States, she studied computer repair at the Milwaukee Area Technical School in Milwaukee, Wisconsin from September 1989 to September 1991 and received a certificate.

EDUCATION	NAME AND LOCATION OF SCHOOL	NO. OF YEARS COMPLETED	DID YOU GRADUATE?	DEGREE RECEIVED
HIGH SCHOOL			☐ Yes ☐ No	
COLLEGE / UNIVERSITY			☑ Yes ☐ No	
TRADE / TECHNICAL SCHOOL			☑ Yes ☐ No	

2. Khamsone went to Thatluang Elementary School in Thatluang, Laos. When he came to the United States, he studied home health care at Caregivers in Atlanta, Georgia, from June 1995 to December 1995 and received a certificate.

EDUCATION					
School	Address	From	To	Did You Graduate?	Subject Studied
Grammar School		████	████	████	████
High School		████			
College					
Other Training					

3. Yao went to High School #7 in Shanghai, China. After she graduated from high school, she attended South China College in Canton, China. She studied mechanical engineering from September 1982 to June 1984 and received an Associate of Science degree.

EDUCATION				
NAME AND ADDRESS OF SCHOOL	From mo. / yr.	To mo. / yr.	CIRCLE HIGHEST GRADE LEVEL COMPLETED	DEGREE / MAJOR
HIGH SCHOOL	✕	✕	9 10 11 12	
COLLEGE			1 2 3 4	
GRADUATE			1 2 3 4	
OTHER			1 2 3 4	

9 ON YOUR OWN

Here is the Education part of a job application. Fill out information about yourself.

EDUCATION	NAME AND LOCATION OF SCHOOL	CIRCLE LAST YEAR COMPLETED	DID YOU GRADUATE?	SUBJECTS STUDIED AND DEGREES RECEIVED
GRAMMAR SCHOOL			☐ Yes ☐ No	
HIGH SCHOOL		1 2 3 4	☐ Yes ☐ No	
COLLEGE / UNIVERSITY		1 2 3 4	☐ Yes ☐ No	
TRADE / TECHNICAL SCHOOL		1 2 3 4	☐ Yes ☐ No	

REFERENCES

On some job applications, you need to fill out information about your references. References are people who know you and can tell a manager about you. On some applications, you need to fill out information about professional references (people who know about your work; for example, supervisors or co-workers). On some applications, you need to fill out information about your personal references (friends). On other applications, you can fill out information about professional *or* personal references.

BE CAREFUL: Relatives (brothers, sisters, aunts, cousins, etc.) *cannot* be references.

HOW TO FILL OUT INFORMATION ABOUT YOUR REFERENCES

You need to fill out some of this information about your references:

- **Your reference's name:** Write the first name and then the family name.
- **Your reference's address:** Write the name of the company and the work address. If your reference is not working, write the home address.
- **Your reference's telephone number:** Write the work telephone number. If your reference is not working, write the home telephone number.
- **Your reference's occupation or position:** Write your reference's job title.
- **Your relationship to your reference:** Write how you know your reference. Is he or she your friend? Was he or she your supervisor or your co-worker?
- **Years acquainted:** Write how long you have known your reference.

10 PAIR WORK

Anna filled out two job applications correctly. Here is one part of each application. She filled in different information on each application. Look at the applications with a partner. How many differences can you find? What information is different?

REFERENCES List three personal or professional references (not related to you).			
NAME and POSITION	ADDRESS	PHONE	YEARS ACQUAINTED
Susan Font, Teacher	Hunter Elementary School 465 West End Ave., New York, NY 10024	(212)395-3305	5 months
Zoran Handzar, Shipping Clerk	Ramon's Shipping Co. 1149 2nd Ave., Seattle, WA 98112	(206)495-3470	1
Frank Duhl, Manager	Smart Toys, 735 5th Ave., #3 San Francisco, CA 94118	(415)386-2493	2

REFERENCES List three persons, other than relatives, who have knowledge of your work experience and/or education.			
Name	Address	Relationship	Phone
1. Susan Font	Hunter Elementary School 465 West End Ave., New York, NY 10024	Friend	(212)395-3305
2. Zoran Handzar	Ramon's Shipping Co. 1149 2nd Ave., Seattle, WA 98112	Friend	(206)495-3470
3. Frank Duhl	Smart Toys, 735 5th Ave., #3 San Francisco, CA 94118	Supervisor	(415)386-2493

11   WORDS FOR SUCCESS

Circle the correct letter to complete each sentence.

1. A _____ knows your skills and experience. He or she can be your supervisor or your co-worker.

    a. professional reference
    b. personal reference

2. A _____ does not know your experience but can talk about your personal qualities and transferable skills. He or she can be a friend.

    a. business reference
    b. personal reference

3. Managers do not want you to use your _____ as references on a job application.

    a. relatives
    b. friends or co-workers

4. People not related to you are your _____.

    a. relatives
    b. friends or co-workers

5. Managers want to know your connection or _____ to your references. Is your reference a friend, a co-worker, or a supervisor?

    a. relative
    b. relationship

6. If you have known your reference for one year, write "1 year" when you read _____.

    a. years employed
    b. years acquainted

CONTACTING YOUR REFERENCES

When you want people to be your references, you need to contact them and ask them some questions before you apply for a job. Ask them if it is okay to use their names as references. You also need to check information about them because you need to fill out applications correctly.

Managers often call your references to learn more about you before they hire you. You should tell your references the job you are applying for because they need to be ready to answer a manager's questions about you.

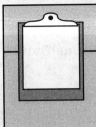

HOW TO ASK SOMEONE TO BE A REFERENCE

When you ask someone to be a reference, you need to do these things:

- Tell him or her the job you are applying for.
- Ask if you can use his or her name as a reference.
- Check the spelling of his or her name.
- Check his or her address.
- Check his or her telephone number, if necessary.

⌒ 12 LISTENING

Listen to a telephone conversation between Nehanda, a job applicant, and her friend, Ashaki. Fill in the blanks.

Ashaki: Hello?

Nehanda: Hi, Ashaki. _____ Nehanda. How are you?

Ashaki: Fine, thanks. And you?

Nehanda: Pretty good. I'm looking for a job as a hospital orderly, and I'm filling out job applications. _____?

Ashaki: Sure.

Nehanda: _____ as a reference?

Ashaki: I'd be happy to be a personal reference.

Nehanda: _____. Let's see. _____ check the spelling of your last name? Is it B–A–K / A–R–I?

Ashaki: That's right.

Nehanda: And _____, please?

Ashaki: 2830 College Avenue.

Nehanda: 2830 College Avenue?

Ashaki: Right.

Nehanda: _____, Ashaki.

Ashaki: You're welcome. And good luck!

Nehanda: Thanks. Goodbye.

Ashaki: Goodbye.

13 PAIR WORK

Work with a partner. Practice the conversation in Exercise 12. When you finish, change roles.

14 APPLY YOURSELF

Ask three people if you can use their names as references. Try to ask people who speak English well. Then write the information about your references on this part of a job application.

REFERENCES				
List the names and address of three people (not relatives) who have known you for at least one year.				
1. Name	Occupation	Relationship		
Address		Telephone	Years Known	
2. Name	Occupation	Relationship		
Address		Telephone	Years Known	
3. Name	Occupation	Relationship		
Address		Telephone	Years Known	

15 ON YOUR OWN

In Unit 5 and this unit, you learned how to fill out job applications with important information about yourself, your work history, your education, and your references. Fill out this **Personal Data Form** with information about yourself. Take this form with you when you go to companies to fill out job applications.

PERSONAL INFORMATION

NAME:_____
              last   first   middle initial

ADDRESS: _____
            street   city   state   ZIP code

PHONE: (   ) _____

SOCIAL SECURITY NUMBER: _____

POSITION OBJECTIVE

POSITION DESIRED _____

DATE AVAILABLE _____

TYPE OF EMPLOYMENT DESIRED   Full-time   Part-time   Permanent   Temporary

DAYS AND HOURS AVAILABLE TO WORK _____

EDUCATION

ELEMENTARY SCHOOL

    Name _____

    Address _____

    Did you finish? _____

HIGH SCHOOL

    Name _____

    Address _____

    Number of Years Attended _____

    Major _____

    Diploma _____

TRADE, TECHNICAL, OR VOCATIONAL SCHOOL

    Name _____

    Address _____

    Dates Attended _____

    Major _____

    Certificate or Degree _____

COLLEGE / UNIVERSITY

    Name _____

    Address _____

    Dates Attended _____

    Major _____

    Degree _____

GRADUATE SCHOOL

    Name _____

    Address _____

    Dates Attended _____

    Major _____

    Degree _____

WORK HISTORY

List your past jobs. Start with your most recent.

1. COMPANY _____
   COMPANY ADDRESS _____
   DATES EMPLOYED _____
   JOB TITLE _____
   JOB DUTIES _____
   _____
   _____
   STARTING SALARY _____ FINAL SALARY _____
   SUPERVISOR'S NAME _____
   REASON FOR LEAVING _____

2. COMPANY _____
   COMPANY ADDRESS _____
   DATES EMPLOYED _____
   JOB TITLE _____
   JOB DUTIES _____
   _____
   STARTING SALARY _____ FINAL SALARY _____
   SUPERVISOR'S NAME _____
   REASON FOR LEAVING _____

3. COMPANY _____
   COMPANY ADDRESS _____
   DATES EMPLOYED _____
   JOB TITLE _____
   JOB DUTIES _____
   _____
   STARTING SALARY _____ FINAL SALARY _____
   SUPERVISOR'S NAME _____
   REASON FOR LEAVING _____

REFERENCES

1. NAME _____

   ADDRESS _____

   PHONE _____

   JOB TITLE _____

   RELATIONSHIP _____

   YEARS KNOWN _____

2. NAME _____

   ADDRESS _____

   PHONE _____

   JOB TITLE _____

   RELATIONSHIP _____

   YEARS KNOWN _____

3. NAME _____

   ADDRESS _____

   PHONE _____

   JOB TITLE _____

   RELATIONSHIP _____

   YEARS KNOWN _____

16 REVIEW

Here is an example of a job application. Fill out information about yourself, the position you want, your education, your work history, and your references. You can use your Personal Data Form on pages 140–143. Print neatly. Use correct punctuation and capitalization.

Application For Employment

PLEASE COMPLETE ALL SECTIONS, EVEN IF YOU ARE ATTACHING A RESUME

NAME: LAST	FIRST	MIDDLE	HOME PHONE NO.

ADDRESS			WORK PHONE NO.

CITY	STATE	ZIP CODE	SOCIAL SECURITY NO.

POSITION DESIRED	SALARY DESIRED	

HAVE YOU EVER BEEN EMPLOYED BY US?

☐ YES ☐ NO IF YES, WHERE?

GENERAL INFORMATION

ARE ANY OF YOUR RELATIVES EMPLOYED BY US?

☐ YES ☐ NO LOCATION

RELATIONSHIP(S)

HAVE YOU BEEN CONVICTED OF ANY FELONY CRIME IN THE LAST SEVEN YEARS?

☐ YES ☐ NO IF YES, EXPLAIN:

ARE YOU UNDER 18 YEARS OF AGE? ☐ YES ☐ NO

DO YOU DESIRE: ☐ FULL-TIME ☐ PART-TIME ☐ TEMPORARY

PLEASE INDICATE THE HOURS THAT YOU ARE AVAILABLE TO WORK ON EACH OF THESE DAYS:

	SUNDAY	MONDAY	TUESDAY	WEDNESDAY	THURSDAY	FRIDAY	SATURDAY
FROM (Hours)							
TO (Hours)							

Should your availability change during the course of your employment, it may impact your employment status based upon our business needs. While we may be able to accommodate your availability limitations upon hire, we do not guarantee that we will be able to support these limitations in the future. Should our business needs change, we may require an adjustment in your availability.

EDUCATION

	SCHOOL NAME	ADDRESS	FROM	TO	DEGREE/DIPLOMA
HIGH SCHOOL					
BUSINESS/VOCATION SCHOOL					
COLLEGE/UNIVERSITY					
COLLEGE/UNIVERSITY					

WORK EXPERIENCE

Application For Employment

COMPANY						PHONE NUMBER	
ADDRESS	STREET		CITY	STATE	ZIP	EMPLOYMENT DATES FROM:	TO:
POSITION HELD						STARTING SALARY	PRESENT/FINAL SALARY
IMMEDIATE SUPERVISOR						DUTIES PERFORMED	
REASON FOR LEAVING							

COMPANY						PHONE NUMBER	
ADDRESS	STREET		CITY	STATE	ZIP	EMPLOYMENT DATES FROM:	TO:
POSITION HELD						STARTING SALARY	FINAL SALARY
IMMEDIATE SUPERVISOR						DUTIES PERFORMED	
REASON FOR LEAVING							

COMPANY						PHONE NUMBER	
ADDRESS	STREET		CITY	STATE	ZIP	EMPLOYMENT DATES FROM:	TO:
POSITION HELD						STARTING SALARY	FINAL SALARY
IMMEDIATE SUPERVISOR						DUTIES PERFORMED	
REASON FOR LEAVING							

REFERENCES

LIST THREE PERSONAL OR ADDITIONAL PROFESSIONAL REFERENCES (NON-FAMILY MEMBERS):	NAME	PHONE NUMBER	YEARS KNOWN	RELATIONSHIP

PLEASE READ CAREFULLY:

All of our employees may be bonded, and a thorough investigation will be made. It is vitally important that all questions be answered accurately as requested. I understand and agree that if hired, my employment may be terminated at any time if I inaccurately provided or omitted information upon completion of this form or when such facts are discovered by my employer.

I hereby certify that my answers to the questions on this application are true and correct to the best of my knowledge. I give you, the employer, or the applicable subsidiary, the right to verify all requested information and to otherwise investigate my qualifications for employment which may include, but not be limited to, securing additional information. I understand that a bonding and security investigation may be made whereby information is obtained through personal interviews with third parties, such as family members, business associates, financial sources, friends, neighbors, or others with whom I am acquainted. I hereby release all persons from any liability in this investigation.

I understand that any offer of employment is conditioned upon the satisfactory completion of this verification process and that the company will hire only those individuals who are legally authorized to work in the United States and who present acceptable proof of their lawful employment status and identity.

APPLICANT'S SIGNATURE _____ DATE _____

FOR COMPANY USE ONLY					
STARTING DATE	SALARY	PAY GRADE	☐ EXEMPT ☐ NON-EXEMPT	DATE JOB OFFERED	DEPARTMENT/STORE NO.
EMPLOYEE NO.	POSITION			HIRED BY	

7003 6/94

FURTEST

WRITING A RESUME

A resume is typed information about your skills, your past jobs, and your education. Some managers will ask you to fill out a job application. Other managers will ask you for a resume. Managers can learn a lot about you from a job application, but they can learn other things about you from a resume because you can write more about your transferable skills on a resume.

A resume is like a job application in some ways. All of the information you write on a resume must be correct and neat. Always check your spelling and your grammar, and ask someone else to check your resume for mistakes.

In some ways, a resume is different from a job application. For example, a resume should be short—only one page. Also, you must type your resume. If you do not have a computer or a typewriter at home, you can go to a copy shop and rent a computer to type your resume or you can pay someone to type it for you.

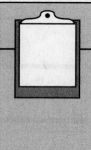

HOW TO WRITE A RESUME

You need to write this information on your resume:

- Your name (first name, then last name), address, and telephone number
- Your work objective: Write the job you want now.
- Your qualifications: Write your skills, qualities, and experience that will help you in the job you are applying for now.
- Your work experience
- Your education
- A sentence about your references

17 ON YOUR OWN

Here is an example of a resume. First, read the resume carefully.

MY THAM
(614) 374-9982

2155 River Road
Columbus, OH 43210

OBJECTIVE: Position as a teacher's assistant

QUALIFICATIONS:

- Five years' teaching experience in kindergarten and elementary school
- Organized, creative, and energetic
- Work well with parents, children, and other teachers

EXPERIENCE:

Elementary School Teacher   1993–1996

Bode Elementary School, Cholon, Vietnam
Taught reading, writing, science, and health to children ages 7–9

Teacher's Assistant   1991–1992

Bode Elementary School, Cholon, Vietnam
Assisted teacher in kindergarten classes

EDUCATION:

Supham University, Saigon, Vietnam
B.A. Elementary Education

References available upon request.

Now, write your own resume. You can use your Personal Data Form on pages 140–143. Remember that you need to type your resume before you give it to a manager.

OBJECTIVE:

QUALIFICATIONS:

-
-
-

EXPERIENCE:

EDUCATION:

References available upon request.

For the test

Writing a Cover Letter

When you send a resume to a manager, you also need to send a cover letter. In a cover letter, you introduce yourself to a manager. You need to write about why you are the best person for the job. Many managers will not read your resume if you do not send a cover letter.

A cover letter should be very short—less than one page. You must type your cover letter, and you need to use a business letter style.

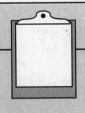

HOW TO WRITE A COVER LETTER

You need to write this information in your cover letter:

- Your name
- Your address
- Today's date
- Manager's name and job title
- Company name and address
- Greeting
  — It's very important to send your cover letter and resume to the person who does the hiring. Be sure to spell the name correctly. If you cannot find out the manager's name, you can write *To Whom It May Concern:*
- Body
  — Give the title of the job you are applying for.
  — Tell how you found out about the job.
  — Say that you are interested in the job.
  — Say that you have enclosed your resume.
  — Write two or three sentences about your experience and/or your transferable skills.
- Closing
  — Thank the manager.
  — Write *Sincerely,*
- Your signature
- Your typed name

18 ON YOUR OWN

Here is an example of a cover letter. First, read the cover letter carefully.

My Tham
2155 River Road
Columbus, OH 43210
(614) 374-9982

February 6, 1996

Edward Rodriguez
Principal
Lowell Elementary School
1488 Taylor Avenue
Columbus, OH 43219

Dear Mr. Rodriguez:

I read your advertisement in last Sunday's *Columbus Post* for a position as a teacher's assistant. I am very interested in this position and have enclosed my resume.

I have five years' experience as an elementary school teacher and teacher's assistant. I know how to organize lessons, and I love to work with children. I am very creative and energetic.

I look forward to hearing from you soon.

Sincerely,

My Tham

My Tham

Now write your own cover letter to Maraya Karena. She is the Personnel Director of the Columbia Company. Her address is 2565 Bowman Avenue, Louisville, Kentucky 40217. You are writing to her about your short-term job goal. Make sure the information you include agrees with the information on your resume in Exercise 17.

Your name, address, and telephone number

_____

_____

_____

_____

Today's date

_____

Employer's name and title

_____

_____

Company name and address

_____

_____

Mr./Ms. + last name

_____:

How you know about the job you are interested in

_____

_____

_____

Your experience and your work skills and personal qualities

_____

_____

_____

I look forward to hearing from you soon.

Sincerely,

Sign your name

Type your name

_____

ENVELOPES

It is important to address an envelope correctly and neatly. Look at this example.

Your name
Your street address
Your city, state, ZIP code

Employer's name
Employer's job title
Company name
Company street address
Company city, state, ZIP code

My Tham
2155 River Road
Columbus, OH 43210

Edward Rodriguez
Principal
Lowell Elementary School
1488 Taylor Avenue
Columbus, OH 43219

19 ON YOUR OWN

You are applying for the job in this want ad. Address an envelope.

MAINTENANCE WORKER,
Mt. Herman Hosp. Exc. bnfts. 1
yr. exper. Send resume: Pavel
Lorca, Personnel Mgr., Mt.
Herman Hosp., 1 Park Ave, Ste
114, San Mateo, CA 94403.

CULTURE NOTES
Getting a Job Is a Full-Time Job

Looking for a job is a full-time job. Sometimes people get jobs quickly, but usually it takes a lot of time to find a job in North America. When you are looking for a job, you need to talk to many managers, fill out many applications, and send many resumes. You need to do the following things.

Beginning your job search:

- Make a long list of companies that might have job openings for you. Use your network, the want ads, "Help Wanted" signs, and job listings.
- Fill out applications for as many companies as you can. You can walk in or call companies to get applications. If a company prefers a resume, send a resume and a cover letter.
- Apply for job openings *immediately*. Don't wait. Sometimes 50, 100, or even 200 people apply for the same job. Managers usually want to hire someone quickly. Managers look carefully at the first applications they receive. Sometimes managers do not even look at applications that arrive late.

Following up: It is very important to follow up after you apply for a job. If you follow up, managers will know that you are really interested in the job you applied for. Call each company or walk in again one or two weeks after you apply for a job. Ask for the manager. You can say:

- "I applied for a job as a nurse's assistant on _____ June 21st _____ ."

                        (job title)   (when you applied)
- "I'm still very interested in the job."
- "Did you have a chance to look at my application / resume ?"

Keeping records: Write down information about each job you apply for immediately after you apply for it. If you apply for many jobs, you might forget important information that you need to follow up on if you don't write it down. Write down this information:

- The date you applied
- How you applied
- The name of the company
- The address of the company
- The telephone number of the company
- The manager's name
- Follow-up information (what you should do next)

20 APPLY YOURSELF

Call or walk into three companies that might have job openings for you. Apply for a job in each company. Fill out job applications or give managers your resume. Then fill in the chart below.

	Company #1	Company #2	Company #3
Date you applied for the job			
How you applied for the job			
Name of company			
Address of company			
Telephone number of company			
Manager's name			
Follow-up information			

21 TEAM WORK

Work in small groups. Discuss the following questions about what you did in Exercise 20.

1. What job(s) did you apply for?

2. How did you apply at each company?

3. Did you talk to the managers? If so, what did each manager say?

4. What do you need to do next?

WHAT DO YOU THINK NOW?

Discuss these questions with your classmates.

1. Is the educational system in this country the same as in your country or different?

2. What information do you need to fill out on job applications?

3. Who can be references for you?
   What information do you need to know about your references?

4. What information do you need to include in a resume?

5. What information do you need to include in a cover letter?

22 REVIEW: Cooperative Crossword Puzzle

INFORMATION GAP: Student A, look at this page. Student B, look at page 217.

There are two different clues for each word. Read your clue to your partner. Listen to your partner's clue. Then choose the correct word from the list. Write it in the spaces.

EXAMPLE: Student A: #1 Down. "You can get this document when you finish technical school."

Student B: #1 Down. "You get this when you study auto repair or cosmetology."

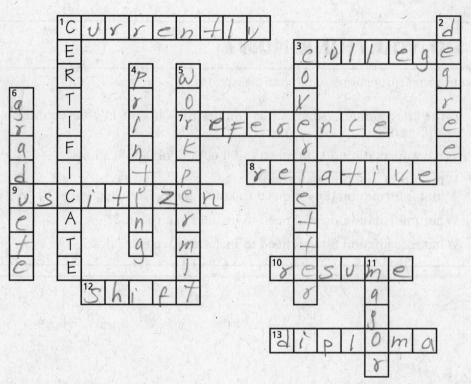

✔ CERTIFICATE
COLLEGE
COVER LETTER
CURRENTLY
DEGREE
DIPLOMA
GRADUATE
MAJOR
PRINTING
REFERENCE
RELATIVE
RESUME
SHIFT
U.S. CITIZEN
WORK PERMIT

DOWN CLUES

1. You can get this document when you finish technical school.
2. You get this when you finish studying in a university.
3. A written introduction to a manager.
4. This is different from handwriting.
5. If you are under 18, you sometimes need to show this to a manager.
6. Finish high school or university.
11. Examples are: engineering, history, mathematics.

ACROSS CLUES

1. Another way to say "now."
3. You can get a bachelor's degree when you finish four years at this kind of school.
7. Examples are: your supervisor, your friend, your co-worker.
8. This person cannot be a reference.
9. This person can get a U.S. passport.
10. This is like a job application in some ways.
12. Your work schedule.
13. You need this document to enter college.

Interviewing: Getting Started

WHAT DO YOU THINK?

Discuss these questions with your classmates.

1. Did you ever have a job interview in your country?
   Did you ever have a job interview in this country?
   What questions did the interviewer (manager) ask you? Give examples.

2. What information do you need to know before you go to an interview?
   What do you need to bring to an interview?

3. How can you make a good impression at a job interview?

4. What are some basic questions an interviewer might ask you during a job interview?

In this unit, you will:

- Learn how to prepare for a job interview.
- Learn how to make a good impression at an interview.
- Learn how to answer basic (simple) interview questions.

PREPARING FOR AN INTERVIEW

It is very important to prepare for a job interview. If you prepare well, the interviewer will know that you are organized and that you are really interested in the job. If you learn as much as you can about the job and the company before the interview, and if you are careful about your appearance, then you will make a good impression. If you practice the interview questions that managers usually ask, then you will feel confident when you speak.

HOW TO PREPARE FOR AN INTERVIEW

Know the time, the place, and how to get there. You need to know this information:

- The date and time of your interview
- The street address and cross street(s)
- The best transportation to the interview (car, train, or bus)
- How long it will take to get to the interview

Know about the interviewer, the job, and the company. You need to know this information:

- The name of the person who will interview you
- The type of business and the name of the company
- Some of the job duties
- The usual salary for the job

Prepare to bring these things to your interview:

- Your Personal Data Form (Unit 6, pages 140–143)
- A typed list of references (names, addresses, telephone numbers)
- Your resume

Think about these things:

- The answers to usual interview questions
- The clothes you will wear (clean and ironed)
- Child care (if you have children)

⌒ 1 LISTENING

You will hear six managers talking about how to prepare for an interview. What is important to each manager? Write the number of the conversation next to the correct sentences.

___ Learn about the job, the company, and the usual salary.

___ Know the address of the company, the date of the interview, and the interviewer's name.

___ Bring information about your work history and education, a list of your references, and your resume.

___ Practice your answers to usual interview questions.

___ Choose the clothes you will wear to an interview when you begin to look for a job, and be sure that you look professional.

___ Arrive at an interview ten or fifteen minutes early, and always go to an interview alone.

2 TEAM WORK

Work in small groups. Read the situations. Then discuss these questions.

How did each applicant prepare for his or her interview?
What did each applicant do well?
What should each applicant do differently next time?
What should each applicant do now?

1. **Maya:** "I got up early because I have an interview at 10:30. Now it's 9:30 and I'm ready to leave. I thought I had a lot of time to get to my interview, but now I see that there is a button missing on my blouse! I don't have anything else to wear for my interview!"

2. **Dean:** "Every morning, I take my daughter to preschool at 10:00. I have an interview at 11:00 today. It's 9:45 now. I just called the company to check the address. I told the receptionist that I had an 11:00 interview. She said, 'No. Your interview is at 10:00.' I have to take my daughter to school now, and my wife is already at work!"

3. **Damon:** "I'm on the bus, and I'm going to my interview. I called the company two days ago to find out the address. It's 1269 Center Avenue. I also called the bus company. A woman told me that I needed forty-five minutes to get to my interview. She told me to take the Center Avenue bus. I left an hour before the interview, and I got on the Center Avenue bus. I'm looking out the bus window now, and I can't see the numbers on the buildings. I don't know where to get off the bus, and my interview is in fifteen minutes!"

4. **Beth:** "My interview is at 2:00. I arrived at the company at 1:45, and I'm filling out a job application now. I remember almost everything—my past job duties, the names of my supervisors, all about my education. But I can't remember the telephone numbers of my references. And I don't really know the addresses of my past supervisors!"

5. **Raul:** "I have an interview at the Marriott Hotel at 3:00 today. Last week, I talked to my friend, Sergio, who works there. He told me about the hotel, his duties, and his salary. It's 2:45. I just arrived at the hotel, but I can't remember the manager's name!"

6. **Sabine:** "I just had an interview, but it didn't go very well. I thought I was prepared. I wore a suit, and I think I looked really nice. I had a list of my references and information about my past jobs and my education. But the manager asked me so many questions, and I didn't know how to answer them! I felt nervous, and I didn't say very much."

CULTURE NOTES
How to Make a Good Impression

An interview is a face-to-face conversation between a job applicant and a manager (interviewer). Talking to a manager at an interview is similar to talking to a manager on the telephone, but an interview is usually much longer than a telephone conversation. In Unit 4, you learned how to make a good impression when you talk to a manager:

- Be confident. Don't sound nervous. Don't speak very softly.
- Be friendly and enthusiastic. Put energy into your voice.
- Be an active listener. When you understand, say, "I see," "Uh-huh," or "Okay." In an interview, you can also nod your head to show that you understand. When you don't understand, ask a question.

In Unit 2, you learned that you need to use good body language when you meet a manager face-to-face:

- Wear professional clothes.
- Smile and make eye contact.
- Shake hands firmly.
- Don't be nervous.

Here are some other things that you can do to make a good impression at a job interview. When you answer a manager's questions, you need to sell yourself:

- Be positive. Say good things about your experience, skills, and qualities.
- Talk only about your transferable skills (the skills and qualities that will help you in the job you are applying for).
- Don't give very short answers. Give examples about your past work or life experience.

🎧 3 LISTENING

You will hear five managers talking about good interviews. What is important to each manager? Write the number of the conversation next to the correct sentence.

___ Be confident. Use good body language.

___ Answer the interviewer's questions completely. Give examples.

___ Don't talk about your personal life.

___ Say good things about yourself and about your past job.

___ Be an active listener. Do not be silent.

Now turn to p. 218 and read the conversations that you just listened to and check your answers. Try to understand the main idea, even if you do not understand every word.

4 PAIR WORK

Work with a partner. Discuss these questions.

1. One interviewer said that you should not talk about your personal life. What does that mean? Give examples.

2. Why is it important to give examples when you answer interview questions? What kind of examples should you give?

3. Why is it important to be an active listener? How can you be an active listener?

4. Why is it important to use good body language in an interview? What are some examples of good body language?

5. Why should you be positive in a job interview? What kinds of things should you say about yourself and your past job or jobs?

⌂ 5 LISTENING

Listen to part of an interview. The applicant and the interviewer both use good, active listening. Fill in the blanks.

Interviewer: Could you tell me a little about your background?

Applicant: _____. Could you say that _____?

Interviewer: Sure. Tell me something about yourself. Where are you from? What kind of work did you do?

Applicant: _____ . Well, I'm from Mexico. I came here six months ago. In Mexico, I was a mechanic for five years.

Interviewer: _____ , good. Let me see, could you tell me a little more about your experience? What kind of tools do you know how to use? What do you know about American cars?

Applicant: _____. Could you _____ , please?

Interviewer: Oh, sorry. Tell me about your experience. What kind of tools can you use? What do you know about American cars?

Applicant: _____ . In my last job, I worked on many different kinds of cars. Sometimes I worked on American cars. And the tools are the same in my country.

Interviewer: _____. Well, this is a part-time, temporary position. Does that sound okay to you?

Applicant: I think so. I understand that this is a part-time job, but _____ "temporary" _____?

Interviewer: Well, this job will not last for a long time. It's a three-month job.

Applicant: Okay, _____. That's fine with me.

6 PAIR WORK

Work with a partner. Practice the conversation in Exercise 5. When you finish, change roles.

7 PAIR WORK

Tell your partner about one of these topics:

- Your work experience
- Your life experience
- Your skills and personal qualities

Be concrete. Give examples. Then listen to your partner talk about one of these topics. Use active listening. Ask questions when you don't understand.

8 LISTENING

Listen to your teacher say these sentences two times. First, your teacher will speak without enthusiasm. Then she or he will speak with enthusiasm. Underline the most important words in each sentence. Then repeat each sentence after your teacher. Be enthusiastic!

1. I loved my last job.
2. That's great.
3. I'm really interested in this position.
4. I'm willing to work very hard.
5. I'd be happy to take an entry-level job.
6. I'm very flexible.
7. I'm learning English very quickly.
8. I have a lot of energy.
9. I work really well with other people.
10. I've heard a lot about your company.

9 PAIR WORK

Work with a partner. Take turns saying the sentences in Exercise 8. Be enthusiastic!

INTRODUCING YOURSELF

When you go to a job interview, you usually need to introduce yourself to the receptionist. After that, you need to introduce yourself to the interviewer. It is important to be friendly and smile when you introduce yourself to both of these people. Remember to shake hands with the interviewer. You do *not* need to shake hands with the receptionist.

HOW TO INTRODUCE YOURSELF AT AN INTERVIEW

When you introduce yourself to a receptionist, you need to do these things:

- Say hello.
- Say your first name, and then your last name.
- Tell the receptionist the name of your interviewer and the time of your appointment.

When you introduce yourself to a manager, you need to do these things:

- Say hello.
- Say your first name, and then your last name.
- Say, "It's nice to meet you."

⌒ 10 LISTENING

You will hear a job applicant introducing himself to a receptionist and to a manager. Fill in the blanks.

Receptionist: Good morning. May I help you?

Applicant: Hello. _____ Doug Marcus.

I _____ Julie Wang _____ ten o'clock.

Receptionist: Could you have a seat, please? I'll tell her that you're here.

Applicant: _____.

Interviewer: Hello. My name is Julie Wang.

Applicant: Hello. _____ Doug Marcus.

It's _____.

Interviewer: It's nice to meet you, too.

11 TEAM WORK

Form groups of three. Practice the conversation in Exercise 10. When you finish, change roles.

CULTURE NOTES
Talking about Money

North Americans usually talk about money *only* with family or good friends. For example, if you do not know someone well, you should *not* ask, "How much money do you make?" or "How much did your car cost?" It is not polite to ask these questions.

In an interview, you also need to be careful when you talk about money. All job applicants want to know about salary, but you should wait for the interviewer to talk about salary. Some interviewers will tell you about salary at the end of an interview. Other interviewers will ask you about the salary you want. Interviewers can ask this question in different ways:

- "What salary are you looking for?"
- "What salary would you like to earn?"
- "What is the minimum wage you will accept?"

Before you go to an interview, it's a good idea to find out the usual salary for the job you are applying for. You can read want ads or talk to friends to learn more about usual salaries.

When the interviewer asks you about salary, do not tell the interviewer the number of dollars that you want. Do not say, for example, "$7.00 an hour." You can answer:

- "I'm open." (I'm flexible about salary.)
- "I'd like the salary you usually pay for this position."
- "I've heard that the usual salary is $7.00 to $10.00 an hour. That's fine for me."

If an interviewer does not tell you about the salary during an interview, you can ask about the salary when the interviewer offers you a job.

12 TEAM WORK

Work in small groups. Discuss these questions.

1. In your country, do people talk about money with their friends and their families? Do people talk about money with people they don't know very well? Give examples.

2. In your country, is it okay to ask people about their rent, their salary, or how much their clothes cost? What money questions *can't* you ask in your country?

3. In your country, how do you find out about the salary for a job you want? Is it okay to ask a manager about salary? If so, when is it okay? If not, how will you find out this information?

BASIC INTERVIEW QUESTIONS

Sometimes interviews are very short. Some interviewers only want to know basic information about you. These interviewers do *not* want to know a lot of information about your past jobs, your skills, or your personal qualities.

BASIC INFORMATION INTERVIEWERS WANT TO KNOW

Interviewers can ask you for this information:

- The work schedule you want
  — The shift you can work
  — The days you can work
  — The hours you can work
- The salary you want
- The type of employment you want
  — Full-time or part-time
  — Permanent or temporary
- Your current work
- Your current supervisor's name and telephone number (if you are working now)
- Your legal right to work
- Your references
- Your experience
- When you can begin to work

🎧 13 LISTENING

You will hear some interviewers asking basic interview questions. Which question do you hear? Circle the correct letter.

1. a. What shift can you work?
   b. What days can you work?
   c. What hours can you work?

2. a. Do you want part-time or full-time employment?
   b. How do you feel about working part-time?
   c. Are you interested in part-time or full-time work?

3. a. What salary are you looking for?
   b. What salary would you like to earn?
   c. What is the minimum wage you will accept?

4. a. Do you want temporary or permanent employment?
   b. This is a temporary job. Is that okay for you?
   c. Are you interested in permanent work?

5. a. When can you start?
   b. What date are you available?
   c. When could you begin working?

6. a. Are you currently employed?
   b. Are you presently working?
   c. Do you have a job right now?

7. a. Could I contact your supervisor?
   b. Could I call your present supervisor?
   c. Could I have the name and number of your current supervisor?

8. a. What position are you interested in?
   b. What job are you applying for?
   c. What kind of work are you looking for?

9. a. Have you done this kind of work before?
   b. Do you have any experience for this job?
   c. What experience do you have for this position?

10. a. Do you have a list of your references?
    b. Could you give me some references?
    c. I'd like to call your references. Can you give me their names and numbers?

14 ON YOUR OWN

Look at these basic interview questions. Then look at the job application below. Match the questions with the information you often read on the job applications. Write the correct number in each circle.

1. What shift can you work?
2. Do you have a list of your references?
3. When can you start?
4. Could I call your supervisor?
5. What salary are you looking for?
6. What job are you applying for?
7. Do you want temporary or permanent employment?
8. Do you have a green card or another proof of your employment eligibility?
9. What days are you available?
10. Do you want full-time or part-time work?
11. Are you working now?

POSITION DESIRED	SALARY DESIRED	DATE AVAILABLE

SHIFT DESIRED
☐ DAY ☐ SWING ☐ NIGHT

TYPE OF EMPLOYMENT DESIRED
☐ FULL-TIME ☐ PART-TIME | ☐ PERMANENT ☐ TEMPORARY

DAYS AVAILABLE

ARE YOU CURRENTLY EMPLOYED?
☐ YES ☐ NO

IF SO, MAY WE CONTACT YOUR PRESENT EMPLOYER? ☐ YES ☐ NO

ARE YOU A U.S. CITIZEN?
☐ YES ☐ NO

IF NOT, ARE YOU LEGALLY ELIGIBLE TO WORK IN THE U.S.? ☐ YES ☐ NO

REFERENCES LIST THREE REFERENCES (NOT RELATED TO YOU)

NAME	PHONE (DAY)	RELATIONSHIP
NAME	PHONE (DAY)	RELATIONSHIP
NAME	PHONE (DAY)	RELATIONSHIP

HOW TO ANSWER BASIC INTERVIEW QUESTIONS

Before you go to an interview, it is important to think about your answers to questions an interviewer can ask you. Here are some ideas to help you prepare good answers:

- **When can you start?** Interviewers usually want job applicants to start work very soon. If you cannot begin to work very soon, you should wait to apply for a job.

- **Do you want permanent or temporary work?** / *Do you want full-time or part-time work? / What schedule can you work (shift/days/hours)?* It is important to be flexible. Sometimes a company does not have the type of job that you want. If you are flexible and you accept *any* position, the company might give you the type of job you want in the future.

- **Are you working now?** If you are working, you should say "Yes" and tell the interviewer where you are working. All of your work experience will help you in a new job.

- **Could I call your supervisor?** It is usually a good idea to say "Yes" because your supervisor can be a reference for you. You should tell your supervisor that you are looking for a new job. If you do not want your supervisor to know that you are looking for a new job, you should explain this to the interviewer.

- **Do you have a list of your references?** When an interviewer asks this question, he or she wants to see your references. You should say "Yes" and give the interviewer your references.

- **What salary are you looking for?** Look at the Culture Notes box on page 164 for information on how to answer this question.

- **Do you have any experience for this job?** Tell the interviewer a little about your experience. If the interviewer asks you for more information about your experience, talk about your past job duties and/or your skills.

15 ON YOUR OWN

Here and on the next page are some questions an interviewer can ask you in an interview. Write the different ways to answer each question, using the answers in the box.

PART A

> I prefer a permanent job, but I'm flexible.
> I'd like to work part-time right now, but I can work full-time in August.
> ✔ I can start immediately.
> I prefer to work Monday to Friday, but anytime is okay.
> I've heard the usual salary is $6.00 to $8.00 an hour. That's fine for me.
> I can start on June 4th.
> I'd like permanent work, but temporary work is okay, too.
> Full-time is better for me, but I'm happy to accept part-time.
> I can work any shift, but I prefer the day shift.
> I'm open.

1. When can you start?

   a. __I can start immediately._____

   b. _____

2. Do you want permanent or temporary work?

   a. _____

   b. _____

3. Do you want full-time or part-time work?

   a. _____

   b. _____

4. What schedule can you work?

   a. _____

   b. _____

5. What salary are you looking for?

   a. _____

   b. _____

PART B

> Yes, Here you are.
> No, I'm not working now.
> Yes, I have three years' experience.
> Yes, her name is Judie Belka. Her number is 542-4610.
> Yes, I'm working at the Corner Cafe.
> I'm sorry. I don't want my supervisor to know that I'm looking for a new job.
> Yes, I worked at the Memorial Hospital for five years.
> Yes, I do. I have it right here.

6. Do you have any experience for this job?

   a. _____

   b. _____

7. Are you working now?

   a. _____

   b. _____

8. Could I call your supervisor?

   a. _____

   b. _____

9. Do you have a list of your references?

   a. _____

   b. _____

LANGUAGE FOCUS
Types of Questions

There are three kinds of questions that an interviewer can ask you:

- Choice questions
- Information questions
- Yes/No questions

Sometimes the interviewer asks you to choose your answer. When the interviewer asks you a choice question (an *or* question), do not say "Yes" or "No." Tell the interviewer what you prefer.

Do you want permanent *or* temporary work? → I prefer permanent work.

Do you want full-time *or* part-time work? → I prefer part-time work.

Sometimes the interviewer asks you for information. When the interviewer asks you an information question (who, what, when, where, how, why), tell the interviewer the information you know.

Who was your supervisor? → David Melbye was my supervisor.

Where did you work? → I worked at Diamond Hair Studio.

When can you start? → Immediately.

What schedule can you work? → Any schedule is fine.

Sometimes the interviewer asks you a Yes/No question. When the interviewer asks you a Yes/No question, answer "Yes" or "No" and give more information.

Do you have any experience for this job? → Yes, I do. I have two years' experience.

Do you have a list of your references? → Yes, I do. Here you are.

Can I call your supervisor? → Yes, you can. Her name is Kathy Demas.

⌒ 16 LISTENING

You will hear some interviewers asking basic questions. Is the interviewer asking a choice question, an information question, or a Yes/No question? Check (✔) the correct answer.

1. __ Choice   __ Information   __ Yes/No
2. __ Choice   __ Information   __ Yes/No
3. __ Choice   __ Information   __ Yes/No
4. __ Choice   __ Information   __ Yes/No
5. __ Choice   __ Information   __ Yes/No
6. __ Choice   __ Information   __ Yes/No
7. __ Choice   __ Information   __ Yes/No
8. __ Choice   __ Information   __ Yes/No

⌒ 17 LISTENING

Listen again to the questions in Exercise 16. What should a job applicant say next? Circle the correct letter.

1. a. Yes, I can. I can work on the weekends.
   b. I can work any shift.
   c. I can start next Monday.

2. a. Yes, I do. I'm available immediately.
   b. Yes, I am. I'm working at Rainbow Cleaners.
   c. Any schedule is fine.

3. a. I prefer full-time, but part-time is okay.
   b. Yes, I do. And I can start tomorrow.
   c. I'm available days or evenings.

4. a. I worked for six years.
   b. No, I didn't work here before.
   c. I worked at the National Bank.

5. a. Yes, I am very interested in this job.
   b. Yes, I have a permanent job.
   c. I prefer permanent work, but I'm flexible.

6. a. I'm sorry. I don't want my supervisor to know I'm looking for a job.
   b. Yes, I do. Here you are.
   c. I'm open, but I've heard that the usual salary is $9.00 to $12.00 an hour.

7. a. Yes, I can work evening hours.
   b. I'm flexible about schedule.
   c. In my last job, I worked ten hours every day.

8. a. I'm open. I'd like the salary you usually pay for this position.
   b. My salary was $8.00 an hour in my last job.
   c. Yes, that's fine for me.

18 PAIR WORK

Create a conversation with a partner. Student A is an interviewer and says the sentences on the left. Student B is a job applicant and follows the directions on the right. Ask questions when you don't understand. When you finish, change roles.

INTERVIEWER	APPLICANT
1. Hello. I'm _____. →	1. Introduce yourself. Say, "Nice to meet you."
2. Nice to meet you, too. What → job are you applying for?	2. Tell the interviewer the job you are applying for.
3. Can you tell me about your → experience?	3. Tell the interviewer about your experience, work skills, personal qualities, or education.
4. What days can you work? →	4. Tell the interviewer the days you can work.
5. What hours can you work? →	5. Tell the interviewer the hours you can work.
6. What salary are you looking → for?	6. Answer the interviewer's question about salary.
7. The salary is $_____ an → hour. Is that okay?	7. Say, "Yes. That's fine."
8. Do you have a list of your → references?	8. Say "Yes." Give the interviewer your references.
9. When can you start? →	9. Tell the interviewer the date you can start.
10. The job starts on _(day)_ at → _(time)_. Are you interested?	10. Say, "Yes." Repeat the day and time. Then say, "Thank you."
11. You're welcome. Goodbye. →	11. Say, "Goodbye."

🎧 19 LISTENING

You will hear two interviews. Write down the information each job applicant receives.

1. Schedule—Days of job: _____

   Schedule—Hours of job: _____

   Full-time or part-time: _____

   Temporary or permanent: _____

   Salary: _____

   Day and date job starts: _____

2. Full-time or part-time: _____

   Schedule—Hours of job: _____

   Schedule—Days of job: _____

   Salary: _____

   Day and date job starts: _____

20 ROLE PLAYS

INFORMATION GAP: Student A, look at this page. Student B, look at page 219.

Work with a partner. Read the first situation. Then create a conversation. When you finish, read the second situation. Create another conversation. Applicants, remember to be enthusiastic, use active listening, and use good body language.

1. You are an interviewer. You are interviewing Student B. Ask, "What job are you applying for?" Ask basic interview questions. For example, "What days can you work?" If you do not remember basic interview questions, look at page 165. Tell the applicant this information about the job:

Full-time	9:00 to 5:00
Temporary	$6.50 an hour
Monday through Friday	Starts on Monday, May 8th

2. You are a job applicant at an interview. Answer the interviewer's questions. Ask questions when you don't understand. Repeat and write down the information the interviewer tells you.

   Notes: _____

   _____

   _____

   _____

21 APPLY YOURSELF

Call or walk into three companies that might have job openings for you. Apply for a job in each company. Fill out job applications or give managers your resume. Then fill in the chart below.

	Company #1	Company #2	Company #3
Date you applied for the job			
How you applied for the job			
Name of company			
Address of company			
Telephone number of company			
Manager's name			
Follow-up information			

22 TEAM WORK

Work in small groups. Discuss the following questions about what you did in Exercise 21.

1. What job(s) did you apply for?

2. How did you apply at each company?

3. Did you talk to the managers? If so, what did each manager say?

4. What do you need to do next?

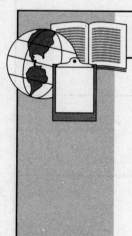

WHAT DO YOU THINK NOW?

Discuss these questions with your classmates.

1. Interviewers know a lot about you from your job application or your resume. Why do they want to interview you?

2. What information do you need to know before you go to an interview?

3. How can you make a good impression at a job interview?

4. What are some basic questions an interviewer might ask you during an interview?

23 REVIEW: Game

Listen to your teacher's instructions. Then play the game.

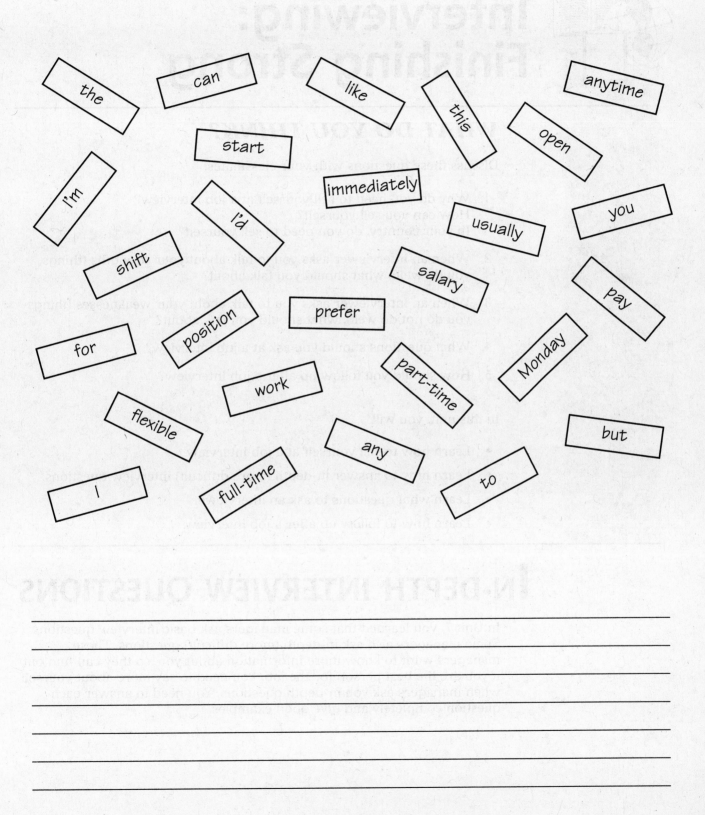

_____

_____

_____

_____

_____

_____

UNIT 8

Interviewing: Finishing Strong

WHAT DO YOU THINK?

Discuss these questions with your classmates.

1. Why do you need to sell yourself at a job interview?
   How can you sell yourself?
   In your country, do you need to sell yourself?

2. When an interviewer asks you to talk about your strengths (things you do well), what should you talk about?

3. When an interviewer asks you to talk about your weaknesses (things you do not do well), what should you talk about?

4. What questions should *you* ask at a job interview?

5. How should you follow up after a job interview?

In this unit, you will:

- Learn how to sell yourself at a job interview.

- Learn how to answer in-depth (more difficult) interview questions.

- Learn what questions to ask an interviewer.

- Learn how to follow up after a job interview.

IN-DEPTH INTERVIEW QUESTIONS

In Unit 7, you learned that some managers ask basic interview questions. Some managers also ask in-depth (more difficult) questions. These managers want to know more information about you, so they can find out if you are the best person for the job. You need to say more about yourself when managers ask you in-depth questions. You need to answer each question completely and give good examples.

🎧 1 LISTENING

You will hear three managers talking about what they want to find out about job applicants in an interview. What is important to each manager? Listen for the main idea. Write the number of the conversation next to the correct sentences.

___ I want to know about applicants' skills and experience.

___ I want to know if applicants really want the job.

___ I want to get to know applicants. I want to know their personal qualities.

🎧 2 LISTENING

Read the phrases below. Then listen again to the managers in Exercise 1. What kind of job applicant does each manager want to hire? Write the number of the conversation next to the correct phrase. Each number can be used more than once.

Applicants who

___ will stay with the company.

___ are confident.

___ will work well with people in the company.

___ are enthusiastic.

___ have the skills they need for the job.

___ are friendly.

CULTURE NOTES
Selling Yourself

In Unit 7, you learned that you need to be confident, friendly, and enthusiastic during a job interview. You also learned that you need to use good body language and be a good listener. It is very important to be positive. You must say good things about yourself in an interview. This is called **selling yourself.**

In everyday life, it is not polite to say many good things about yourself. But in a job interview, the rules of the game are different. There are usually many people applying for one job. When managers ask you in-depth questions, you need to show the interviewer that *you* are the best person for the job. You can do this by selling yourself. Getting a job is similar to a sports competition. There is one winner.

Selling yourself is also like selling a product. When salespeople sell their products, they need to be enthusiastic. They need to give examples, so customers can see that their product is the best.

You need to sell yourself to an interviewer. You should tell the interviewer how you can help the company. You should give good examples of your experience, personal qualities, and skills. You should be enthusiastic about the job you are applying for, so the interviewer knows that you really want the job.

3 TEAM WORK

Work in small groups. Each group will choose one product that you all know well (such as toothpaste, candy, or a bicycle). Talk to the people in your group about how you can "sell" this product. What are the good things about this product? Why will someone buy it? Give examples.

EXAMPLE

"This is a great house. It is very big, but the rent is not expensive. There are four bedrooms, a large kitchen, two bathrooms, and a beautiful backyard with a garden. It is very sunny because there are a lot of windows. It is also clean. We just painted the walls, and the carpet is new. The neighborhood is very quiet, and there are many stores nearby. You will never want to leave this house!"

What product will your group sell? _____

What examples will help you sell this product? _____

_____

_____

_____

4 TEAM REPORTS

Sell your product from Exercise 3 to your class. Be enthusiastic and positive! Listen to the other groups sell their products.

5 ON YOUR OWN

Read the sentences. Circle the letter of the answer that is the most positive in each pair.

1. Interviewer: Can you tell me about yourself?

   a. I want to be an automobile body repair person, but I don't have any experience in this country. In my last job I repaired cars, but all the cars are different here.
   b. In my country, I worked as an automobile body repair person at a garage. I repaired many kinds of cars, and I used different tools. My past experience will help me in a job here.

2. Interviewer: Do you have any experience working in a photo lab?

   a. No, I don't. I was a student. I was studying to be a doctor, but I had to leave my country.
   b. Well, I took photography classes at the university. I worked in the photo lab there every week.

3. Interviewer: Can you type?

   a. Yes, and I'm studying typing at the adult school now. My typing skills are improving.

   b. Yes, but I type very slowly, and I make many mistakes.

4. Interviewer: Do you have any experience as a stock clerk?

   a. No, but I worked in a store for a year. I was a cashier, and I'm very good with numbers.

   b. No, I've never worked as a stock clerk before. I was a secretary in my last job.

5. Interviewer: What job are you interested in?

   a. Well, I'm applying for a job as an orderly now, but I really want to be an engineer.

   b. I'm applying for a job as an orderly. I'm really interested in working at your hospital.

TELLING AN INTERVIEWER ABOUT YOURSELF

At the beginning of an interview, interviewers usually want to know a little about you (your background). Your answer should be similar to your telephone introduction to the manager. Interviewers do *not* want to know about your family or your personal problems.

Interviewers may ask this question in different ways:

Can you tell me about yourself?
Could you tell me about your background?

HOW TO TELL AN INTERVIEWER ABOUT YOURSELF

When you have experience for the job you want, you should tell the interviewer this information about yourself:

- The job you want now
- Your past job title
- One or two sentences about your experience

When you do *not* have experience for the job you want, you should tell the interviewer this information about yourself:

- The job you want now
- Your past job title
- One or two sentences about your work skills, your personal qualities, or your education that will help you in your job

🎧 6 LISTENING

You will hear five applicants answering the question, "Can you tell me about yourself?" What information does each applicant tell the interviewer? Check (✔) the boxes.

	1	2	3	4	5
The job he or she wants now					
His or her past job title					
One or two sentences about his or her experience, skills, personal qualities, or education					

🎧 7 LISTENING

Listen again to the conversations in Exercise 6. Discuss these questions with your classmates.

1. In which conversations did the applicants give good answers?

2. In which conversations did the applicants make mistakes?

3. What did they do wrong?

8 ON YOUR OWN

Write your answer to the interview question, "Can you tell me about yourself?"

EXAMPLE   "My name is Neora Tieng. I'm from Cambodia. Now I would like to work as a cashier. In my last job, I was a postal clerk. I know how to collect money and give change. I'm very good with numbers."

My name is _____. I'm from _____.
             (your name)   (your country)

Now I would like to work as _____.
             (job you are applying for)

In my last job, I was _____.
             (past job title)

I worked at _____ for _____ years.
       (kind of company)   (number)

I _____
        (one or two sentences about your experience,

_____.
        skills, personal qualities, or education)

9 PAIR WORK

Work with a partner. Practice your answer in Exercise 8. Remember to be enthusiastic, to be confident, and to use good body language.

TELLING AN INTERVIEWER ABOUT YOUR EXPERIENCE

After you tell the interviewer about yourself, the interviewer will often ask you to say more about your experience. In Unit 4, you learned how to talk about your experience to a manager on the telephone. In an interview, your answer should be similar to your answer on the telephone, but you need to say *more* about your experience.

You need to give examples. Be *concrete* and *positive*. Tell the interviewer about your past job duties, skills, and personal qualities that will help you in the job you are applying for.

You can also tell the interviewer about your education, but talk only about special courses or a certificate you received that will help you in your new job.

Interviewers may ask this question in different ways:

Can you tell me about your experience?
Could you tell me about your last job or jobs?
What were your major responsibilities in your last job?
What were your main duties in your last job?
What kind of experience do you have that will help you in this job?

HOW TO TELL AN INTERVIEWER ABOUT YOUR EXPERIENCE

When you have experience in the job you are applying for, you should tell the interviewer this information:

- More about your past job duties
- Examples of your past job duties

When you do not have experience in the job you are applying for, you should tell the interviewer this information:

- More about your transferable skills (work skills, life skills, and personal qualities)
- Examples of your transferable skills

🎧 10 LISTENING

You will hear five job applicants answer the question, "Can you tell me about your experience?" Does each applicant give examples of his or her experience? Circle *Yes* or *No*.

Applicant # 1	Yes	No
Applicant # 2	Yes	No
Applicant # 3	Yes	No
Applicant # 4	Yes	No
Applicant # 5	Yes	No

11   TEAM WORK

Work in small groups. Talk about a usual day in your last job. Be concrete. Give examples of your job duties. Then listen to your classmates talk about their jobs.

12   ON YOUR OWN

Read two job applicants' answers to the question, "Can you tell me about your experience?"

APPLICANT 1

Telephone answer:

"In my last job, I was a painter. I painted inside and outside apartments and offices. I removed paint from walls. I used paint brushes and ladders."

Interview answer:

"In my last job, I was a painter. I had a small painting business with my brother and my son for twelve years. Most of our work was inside offices and apartment buildings.

"In the summer, we also painted the outsides of buildings. For example, last summer we painted a large apartment building. It was very old, so we needed to remove all of the old paint. We also needed to repair the windows before we painted. It was a big job, but we worked on the weekends, too, and finished it in three weeks.

"The owner of the apartment liked our work because we were very efficient and careful with details. He told his friend, and we got another big job after that. We always had a lot of business because we are hard workers."

APPLICANT 2

Telephone answer:

"In my last job, I was a travel agent. I know how to read maps and follow directions. I'm a very careful driver. I'm efficient, and I work well under pressure."

Interview answer:

"In my last job, I was a travel agent, so I read maps every day. Drivers need to read maps and find the fastest way to get places.

"My customers often needed tickets and information quickly, and I could always help them. June was the busiest month in my office. In one week, I made plans for more than 100 people. One day, the president of a very important company in my city needed to go to El Salvador immediately for a business meeting. I made a lot of telephone calls to get him a plane ticket, a car to rent, and a room in a hotel. I'm very efficient, and I work well under pressure. Drivers need to be efficient, and they work under pressure, too. They need to drive to many places in a short time.

"I'm a very careful driver. I got my driver's license when I was eighteen years old, so I have a lot of experience. Drivers need to be careful and experienced."

13 PAIR WORK

Work with a partner. Discuss these questions about the examples you read in Exercise 12.

1. How are the applicants' interview answers different from their telephone answers?

2. What information does each applicant add to his or her interview answer?

14 ON YOUR OWN

Copy your telephone answer to the question, "Could you tell me more about your experience?" from Unit 4, page 92. Then write your interview answer to the question, "Can you tell me about your experience?" Be concrete. Give examples. Remember to use the past tense for past job duties.

YOUR TELEPHONE ANSWER:

_____

_____

_____

_____

_____

YOUR INTERVIEW ANSWER:

_____

_____

_____

_____

_____

_____

_____

_____

_____

_____

15   PAIR WORK

Work with a partner. Practice your interview answer in Exercise 14. Remember to be enthusiastic, to be confident, and to use good body language.

16   TEAM WORK

Work in groups of three. Each person in your group will play each role one time.

Interviewer: You will ask a job applicant these questions: Can you tell me about yourself? Can you tell me about your experience?

Job applicant: An interviewer will ask you questions. You will answer his or her questions. Remember: Be concrete, confident, and enthusiastic. Use good body language.

Observer: You will observe and listen to the applicant. Answer the questions below. Check (✔) Yes or No.

	Yes	No
Does the applicant say his or her current or past job title?		
Does the applicant say the job he or she wants?		
Does the applicant give concrete examples of his or her experience?		
Does the applicant talk about his or her transferable skills if he or she does not have experience for the job he or she wants?		
Is the applicant enthusiastic?		
Is the applicant confident?		
Does the applicant use good body language?		

TELLING AN INTERVIEWER ABOUT YOUR STRENGTHS

Interviewers will often ask about your strengths. When interviewers ask you about your strengths, they want to know about your best personal qualities and your best work skills. Interviewers are asking you to sell yourself (say good things about yourself).

The question, "What are your strengths?" is different from the question, "Can you tell me about your experience?" When you talk about your strengths, do *not* talk about all of your experience in general. You need to choose two or three of your best personal qualities and/or best work skills and give examples. Choose the strengths that are the most important for the job you want.

Interviewers may ask this question in different ways:

What are your greatest strengths?
What are your strongest points?
What are your best work abilities and best qualities?
Why should I hire you?

HOW TO TELL AN INTERVIEWER ABOUT YOUR STRENGTHS

When you answer the question, "What are your greatest strengths?" you should tell the interviewer this information:

- Your best personal qualities
- Your best work skills
- Examples of your qualities and skills

∩ 17 LISTENING

You will hear five job applicants answer the question, "What are your greatest strengths?" Does each applicant give examples of his or her strengths? Circle *Yes* or *No*.

Applicant # 1	Yes	No
Applicant # 2	Yes	No
Applicant # 3	Yes	No
Applicant # 4	Yes	No
Applicant # 5	Yes	No

∩ 18 LISTENING

You will hear three of the job applicants from Exercise 17 talking about their strengths again. Write the strengths you hear them talk about.

1. _____

2. _____

3. _____

19 ON YOUR OWN

Read about some people who are preparing for job interviews. Then read about their personal qualities and work skills. Which personal qualities and work skills should they talk about in their interviews? Write a number from 1 to 6 next to each personal quality or work skill. (1 is the most important; 6 is not important.) There may be more than one correct answer.

1. Sergei was an electrical engineer. He is applying for a job as a maintenance worker. These are Sergei's strengths:

___ He can design electrical machines.

___ He is organized.

___ He can repair furniture.

___ He can use electrical tools.

___ He is flexible.

___ He is a good problem solver.

2. Jared is a student. He is applying for a job as a security guard. These are Jared's strengths:

___ He is organized.

___ He is a fast learner.

___ He can follow directions.

___ He can take notes.

___ He is creative.

___ He is efficient.

3. Angela stayed home and took care of her house, children, and parents. She is applying for a job as a home health aide. These are Angela's strengths:

___ She is patient.

___ She can care for old people.

___ She can cook.

___ She is reliable.

___ She can care for children.

___ She is creative.

4. Elena was a factory worker. She is applying for a job as a general office clerk. These are Elena's strengths:

___ She is careful with details.

___ She is good with her hands.

___ She can put small pieces together.

___ She can do routine work.

___ She can use a computer.

___ She works well with people.

20 TEAM WORK

Work in small groups. Compare your answers in Exercise 19. Do you agree or disagree with each other? Why? Talk about the most important transferable skills in each situation.

21 TEAM WORK

Work in small groups. In Exercise 3, you chose a product to sell. Now you will practice "selling" your classmates. Talk about one person in your group. What is his or her short-term job goal? What are his or her transferable skills (personal qualities and skills)? How can you "sell" that person to the interviewer? Repeat the activity for each person in your group.

EXAMPLE

"Kim Eng is a fantastic sales clerk. She's very energetic. In her last job, she worked in the toy department at a big store. Her store was very busy, so she talked to many people every day. She is really friendly. Her customers liked her a lot. They asked for Kim when they went to the toy department because she helped them find the best toys. Give Kim a job, and more customers will come to your store."

22 TEAM REPORTS

Choose one person from your group in Exercise 21 and "sell" him or her to your class. Give examples. Be enthusiastic and positive! Listen to the other groups "sell" their group members.

23 ON YOUR OWN

Read a job applicant's answers to the questions, "Can you tell me about your experience?" and "What are your strengths?"

Can you tell me about your experience?

"In my last job, I was a travel agent, so I read maps every day. Drivers need to read maps and find the fastest way to get places.

"My customers often needed tickets and information quickly, and I could always help them. June was the busiest month in my office. In one week, I made plans for more than 100 people. One day, the president of a very important company in my city needed to go to El Salvador immediately for a business meeting. I made a lot of telephone calls to get him a plane ticket, a car to rent, and a room in a hotel. I'm very organized, and I work well under pressure. Drivers need to be organized, and they work under pressure, too. They need to drive to many places in a short time.

"I'm a very careful driver. I got my driver's license when I was eighteen years old, so I have a lot of experience. Drivers need to be careful and experienced."

What are your strengths?

"As I said, I am very careful with details, and I work well under pressure. I never forget important information. I can remember many different things at the same time; for example, names, addresses, and what people need. As a driver for your restaurant, I may have five different deliveries at the same time. I need to remember the customers' names and addresses, and I need to plan the best way to get from one place to another. This is a lot of pressure, but that's okay with me. When I was busy in my last job, I was relaxed, and I always met my deadlines. I also have a lot of experience as a driver. My brother is disabled and I drove him everywhere he needed to go for many years. I'm an excellent driver, so I really think that I will be the best person for this job."

24   PAIR WORK

Work with a partner. Discuss these questions about the examples in
Exercise 23.

1. What examples does the applicant give in each answer?

2. In which answer does the applicant say more about personal qualities
   or skills?

3. In which answer does the applicant talk more about past job duties?

25   ON YOUR OWN

Copy your interview answer to the question, "Could you tell me about
your experience?" from Exercise 14 on page 185. Then write your answer
to the question, "What are your strengths?" Be concrete. Give examples.

YOUR EXPERIENCE:

_____

_____

_____

_____

_____

_____

_____

_____

YOUR STRENGTHS:

_____

_____

_____

_____

_____

_____

_____

26 PAIR WORK

Work with a partner. Practice your interview answer in Exercise 25. Remember to be enthusiastic, to be confident, and to use good body language.

TELLING AN INTERVIEWER ABOUT YOUR WEAKNESSES

Interviewers often ask you about your weaknesses. When interviewers ask about your weaknesses, they want to know if you need to improve any of your skills. They also want to know if you have any negative personal qualities.

Interviewers may ask this question in different ways:

What is your biggest weakness?
What is your weakest point?
What part of your work needs the most improvement?

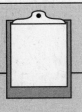

HOW TO TELL AN INTERVIEWER ABOUT YOUR WEAKNESSES

When you talk about your weakness, you should always be positive. You should do these things:

- Talk about a weakness that is already clear to the interviewer.

or

- Talk about a personal quality or a skill that you are improving and how you are improving it.

BE CAREFUL:

- Do *not* talk about a personal quality or skill that is very important for the job you are applying for.
- Tell the interviewer about only *one* weakness. Be honest, but do not say too much about your weakness.
- Do not say, "I don't have any weaknesses." The interviewer will think you are not honest.

27   TEAM WORK

Work with a partner. Read these examples of good and bad answers to the question, "What are your weaknesses?" Talk about why the second answer in each pair is better.

1. Do *not* say: "I don't know how to use a computer."

   You *can* say: "In my last job, I was a cashier. We didn't have a computer in our store, but I type very well, and I'm a fast learner. I am taking a computer class at the community college now."

2. Do *not* say: "I don't know how to use the copy machines you have here."

   You *can* say: "I don't know how to use the copy machines you have here, but I learn quickly. When I was an office clerk, we had a copy machine in our office. I used it often, but it was very old. I also follow instructions very well. I'm sure I'll have no problem using your copy machines."

3. Do *not* say: "My English is very poor."

   You *can* say: "English is my second language. I've only been in this country for six months, but I'm learning English very quickly. I'm taking classes, and I practice speaking English every day."

28   PAIR WORK

Read the sentences. Circle the letter of the most positive answer to each question.

1. Interviewer: What is your weakest point?

   a. I don't have any experience as a busperson. I've never worked in a restaurant before. I was a secretary in a dentist's office.
   b. I don't have any experience as a busperson, but I was a secretary in my last job, and I'm very efficient and organized.

2. Interviewer: What part of your work needs the most improvement?

   a. I want to be a cook, but I don't know the measurement system in this country. People use teaspoons and cups here. We use grams and liters. It's a different measurement system.
   b. I want to be a cook, but I don't know the American measurement system. I don't think this will be a problem because I have a lot of cooking experience, and I'm very good at math. I'm sure I can learn the new system easily.

3. Interviewer: What are your weaknesses?

   a. Sometimes our store was very busy. Many customers asked me questions at the same time, but I couldn't answer all of their questions. Sometimes customers were angry. But I am learning how to solve this problem. For example, I can politely ask one person to wait and answer another person's question. I try to be very patient.

   b. My last supervisor told me that I need to be more patient, but sometimes I can't. It is difficult when there are too many customers in a store. I don't like to answer so many questions. Then I am not patient. I don't like stupid questions, do you? One day, a man asked me, "Where is the soap?" and he was standing next to the soap! Can you believe it?

4. Interviewer: What are your weakest points?

   a. I was an electrician in my last job. Sometimes the work was boring, so I worked slowly and took a lot of breaks. And sometimes I needed to go home early because I have four children. I think you can understand my problem.

   b. I was an electrician in my last job. My weakness is that I don't really have experience as a computer technician. But I'm very good with my hands. I just finished a course in computer repair, and I did very well. My teacher said I am a very fast learner.

🎧 29 LISTENING

You will hear five job applicants answer the question, "What is your biggest weakness?" Does each applicant talk about his or her weakness in a positive way? Circle *Yes* or *No*.

Applicant #1	Yes	No
Applicant #2	Yes	No
Applicant #3	Yes	No
Applicant #4	Yes	No
Applicant #5	Yes	No

🎧 30 LISTENING

Listen again to the conversations in Exercise 29. Discuss these questions with your classmates.

1. In which conversations did the applicants give good answers?

2. In which conversations did the applicants make mistakes?

3. What did they do wrong?

31 ON YOUR OWN

Write your answer to the interview question, "What is your biggest weakness?"

EXAMPLE "I worked in a photo lab before, but I never used the equipment that you have in your company. But I'm a fast learner, and I'm very good with my hands. I love learning how to use new machines, and I am studying photography at the community college now. I'm sure I'll be able to use the equipment you have here very soon."

YOUR WEAKNESS:

_____

_____

_____

_____

32 PAIR WORK

Work with a partner. Practice your interview answer in Exercise 31. Remember to be enthusiastic, to be confident, and to use good body language.

TELLING AN INTERVIEWER ABOUT YOUR CAREER GOALS

Interviewers often ask about your career goals. They want to know your plans for the future because they do not want to hire someone who will leave the company very soon. Companies spend a lot of time and money hiring and training new workers.

Sometimes your long-term goal is similar to your short-term goal (the job you are applying for). Then you can tell the interviewer that you want to work in an entry-level position and grow with the company.

When people want to grow with a company, they plan to stay in *one* company for a long time. They would like to move up step-by-step from an entry-level position to a higher position in the same company.

Sometimes you will want to study and work at the same time. You will *not* want to grow with a company. You will want to move to a different company and a different kind of job when you finish your studies. When your short-term goal and long-term goal are in different companies, you need to tell the interviewer about your plans. You can tell the interviewer that you want to study and work at the same time. It is also very important to tell the interviewer that you will not leave his or her company soon.

Interviewers may ask this question in different ways:

What are your career goals?
What are your goals for the next few years?
What are your plans for the future?
What would you like to be doing in three to five years?

HOW TO TELL AN INTERVIEWER ABOUT YOUR CAREER GOALS

When your short-term goal and long-term goal are similar, you should tell the interviewer this information:

- Your long-term goal
- How you will improve your skills
- That you want to grow with the company (stay at the company)

When your short-term goal and long-term goal are different, you should tell the interviewer this information:

- Your long-term goal
- How you will improve your skills
- That you will not leave the company soon

🎧 33 LISTENING

You will hear five job applicants answer the question, "What are your career goals?" What information does each applicant tell the interviewer? Check (✔) the correct boxes.

	1	2	3	4	5
His or her long-term goal					
How he or she will improve his or her skills					
He or she will not leave the company soon					

🎧 34 LISTENING

Listen again to the conversations in Exercise 33. Discuss these questions with your classmates.

1. In which conversations did the applicants give a good answer?

2. In which conversations did the applicants make mistakes?

3. What mistakes did they make?

35 ON YOUR OWN

Write your answer to the question, "What are your career goals?"

EXAMPLE 1: "Now I'd like to work as a baggage porter in your hotel. I'd really like to grow with your company. I'd like to stay with your hotel. And in three or four years, I would like to work as a front desk clerk, if possible. I plan to keep studying English, and I want to improve my computer skills."

EXAMPLE 2: "Right now I'd like to work as a cashier in your store. I plan to study accounting at the community college at night at the same time. In two or three years, I hope to work as an accountant."

YOUR CAREER GOALS:

_____

_____

_____

_____

36 PAIR WORK

Work with a partner. Practice your interview answer in Exercise 35. Remember to be enthusiastic, to be confident, and to use good body language.

37 TEAM WORK

Make groups of three. Each person in your group will play each role one time.

Interviewer: You will ask a job applicant these questions: What are your greatest strengths? What is your biggest weakness? What are your career goals?

Job applicant: An interviewer will ask you questions. You will answer his or her questions. Remember: Be concrete, positive, and enthusiastic. Use good body language.

Observer: You will observe and listen to the applicant. Answer the questions below. Check (✔) *Yes* or *No*.

	YES	NO
Does the applicant give concrete examples of his or her strengths?		
Does the applicant say positive things about his or her weakness?		
Does the applicant say his or her long-term goal?		
Does the applicant say he or she will not leave the company soon?		
Is the applicant enthusiastic?		
Is the applicant confident?		
Does the applicant use good body language?		

38 ON YOUR OWN

Here and on the next page are some questions an interviewer can ask you. Write the different ways to ask the same questions, using the questions in the boxes.

PART A

> Could you tell me about your last job?
> What would you like to be doing in three to five years?
> What were your major responsibilities in your last job?
> ✔ Could you tell me about your background?
> What kind of experience do you have that will help you in this job?
> What are your plans for the future?
> Tell me a little about yourself.
> What were your main duties in your last job?
> What are your goals for the next few years?

1. Can you tell me about your background?

    a. _Could you tell me about your background?_

    b. _____

2. Can you tell me about your experience?

    a. _____

    b. _____

    c. _____

    d. _____

3. What are your career goals?

    a. _____

    b. _____

    c. _____

PART B

> What are your strongest points?
> What is the minimum wage you will accept?
> What are your best work abilities and best qualities?
> What part of your work needs the most improvement?
> What salary would you like to earn?
> Why should I hire you?
> What is your weakest point?

4. What salary are you looking for?

    a. _____

    b. _____

5. What are your greatest strengths?

    a. _____

    b. _____

    c. _____

6. What is your biggest weakness?

    a. _____

    b. _____

⌒ 39 LISTENING

Read the interview questions below and on the next page. Then listen to a different interview question on the tape. Listen for the important words. Does the question you hear have the same meaning as the question you read? Circle *Same* or *Different*.

1. What were your major responsibilities in your last job?   Same   Different

2. What salary would you like to earn?   Same   Different

3. What are your career goals?   Same   Different

4. Why should I hire you?   Same   Different

5. What are your goals for the next few years?   Same   Different

6. Can you tell me a little about yourself?   Same   Different

7. What is the minimum wage you will accept?   Same   Different

8. What part of your work needs the most improvement?   Same   Different

9. What are your best work abilities and best qualities?   Same   Different

10. What were your main duties in your last job?   Same   Different

---

CULTURE NOTES
Personal Questions

Sometimes interviewers ask personal questions. These questions are *not* about your skills, your strengths, or the job you are applying for. There are some personal questions that interviewers should *not* ask. For example, interviewers should not ask you questions about these topics:

- Your exact age
- Your race, nationality, or religion
- Your health or any physical disability (unless you could not do the job you are applying for because of a disability)
- If you are married
- If you have children

Most interviewers ask applicants personal questions because they want to be friendly. They ask these questions to make you feel comfortable in an interview.

Some interviewers ask applicants personal questions because they do not want to hire certain kinds of people even if these people have the best skills for the job. This is discrimination. For example, maybe an interviewer does not want to hire a working mother because he or she thinks a person with children will not work hard. This interviewer may ask, "Do you have children?" If an interviewer does not hire this applicant *only* because she has children, the interviewer is discriminating against this applicant.

It is illegal to discriminate against job applicants, but it is very hard to prove that an interviewer discriminated against a job applicant.

Most job applicants answer personal questions. If you do not answer an interviewer's questions, he or she may think that you are not polite or that you are hiding some information about yourself.

If an interviewer asks you a personal question, you can:

- Give a short answer to the question.
- Then immediately talk about your strengths or your experience.

40 ON YOUR OWN

Here are some personal questions that interviewers should *not* ask you.
How will you answer each question if an interviewer asks you? Write
your answer.

EXAMPLE Do you have any children?

Yes, I do. I have two children, but I'm very comfortable working
full-time and taking care of my children at the same time. I'm
very reliable. In my last job, I was always on time. If I had more
work than usual, I stayed late and finished it before I went home.

1. I see that English is your second language. What nationality are you?

   _____

   _____

   _____

2. Could you tell me about your family?

   _____

   _____

   _____

CLOSING THE INTERVIEW:
The Questions You Ask

When an interviewer asks, "Do you have any questions for me?" you know
that the interview is almost finished. You should ask the interviewer some
questions about the company and about the job. Then the interviewer
knows that you are really interested in the job. You should ask two or
three questions.

Sometimes the interviewer does not ask, "Do you have any questions for
me?" It is still important to ask the interviewer questions. Then you need
to ask the interviewer, "Could I ask you a few questions?"

If the interviewer did not tell you basic information about the job
(schedule, when the job starts, etc.), you can ask for this information at the
end of an interview.

HOW TO ASK QUESTIONS AT AN INTERVIEW

When an interviewer asks you if you have any questions, you can ask him or her questions about these things:

- Basic information about the job (the schedule, when the job starts, etc.) if the interviewer did not tell you this information
- The job and the company
- When he or she will make a decision and what you should do next\

41 ON YOUR OWN

First, read an example of questions applicants can ask an interviewer.

1. You are applying for a job as a nurse's assistant in a large hospital. The job is on the maternity ward (the place in a hospital where women have babies).

   Job title: Nurse's Assistant
   Workplace: Hospital

   You can ask: Could you tell me about a usual work day?
                  How many people work in the maternity ward?
                  How many babies are born here each week?
                  How many patients does a nurse's assistant usually take care of?

Now, think about your short-term goal. Write the job title of the job you think you will apply for. Write where you think you will work. Write five questions that you can ask at the end of an interview.

Job title: _____

Workplace: _____

1. _____

2. _____

3. _____

4. _____

5. _____

CLOSING THE INTERVIEW: Saying Goodbye

When an interviewer thanks you for coming in, you know that this is the end of the interview. You still need to find out what will happen next and how to follow up after the interview. When will you know if you got the job? Will the interviewer call you or write to you? Do you need to call the interviewer?

Before you say, "Goodbye," you need to thank the interviewer and shake hands again. Remember to use good body language. Smile, make eye contact, and be friendly.

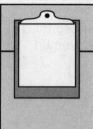

HOW TO SAY GOODBYE TO AN INTERVIEWER

Before you leave an interview, you need to do these things:

- Say, "It was nice to meet you."
- Ask when the interviewer will make a decision.
- Ask if you should contact the interviewer.

∩ 42 LISTENING

You will hear the end of an interview. Fill in the blanks.

Interviewer: Thank you for coming in.

Applicant: It was very _____.

Interviewer: It was nice to meet you, too.

Applicant: When do you think _____?

Interviewer: Well, probably next Thursday or Friday.

Applicant: Okay. Should I _____

me?

Interviewer: I'll contact you.

Applicant: _____.

Interviewer: You're welcome.

Applicant: Goodbye.

Interviewer: Goodbye.

43 PAIR WORK

Practice the conversation in Exercise 42 with a partner. When you finish, change roles.

44 TEAM WORK: Interview Review

You and your classmates will form two circles. Circle 1 is inside Circle 2. The students in Circle 1 are interviewers. They will choose three questions from the list below to ask a job applicant. The students in Circle 2 are job applicants. They will answer the interviewer's questions. Introduce yourselves and shake hands before you begin your interview.

When your teacher tells you to change partners, close the interview and shake hands. All of the applicants in Circle 2 will move to the right one seat. Repeat the activity several times.

Then your teacher will tell you to change roles. Now the students in Circle 1 are job applicants and the students in Circle 2 are interviewers. Repeat the activity several times.

1. Tell me a little about yourself.
   Can you tell me about yourself?
   Could you tell me about your background?

2. Can you tell me about your experience?
   Could you tell me about your last job?
   What were your major responsibilities in your last job?
   What were your main duties in your last job?
   What kind of experience do you have that will help you in this job?

3. What are your career goals?
   What would you like to be doing in three to five years?
   What are your plans for the future?
   What are your goals for the next few years?

4. What salary are you looking for?
   What is the minimum wage you will accept?
   What salary would you like to earn?

5. What are your greatest strengths?
   What are your strongest points?
   What are your best work abilities and best qualities?
   Why should I hire you?

6. What is your biggest weakness?
   What is your weakest point?
   What part of your work needs the most improvement?

FOLLOW-UP: Thank-You Letter

After you have a job interview, you should write a **thank-you letter** immediately. A thank-you letter will show the interviewer that you are really interested in the job. It also thanks the interviewer for the time he or she took to interview you.

- A thank-you letter should be typed.

- A thank-you letter should be written to the interviewer. You need to know the interviewer's first and last name, and you need to spell the interviewer's name correctly. (You can ask for the interviewer's business card at the end of an interview.)

Remember, business letters have a special style. Look at the example of the cover letter in Unit 6 on page 150.

45 ON YOUR OWN

Here is an example of a thank-you letter. First, read it carefully.

Gloria Alonso
722 Greenleaf St.
Wilmette, IL 60091
(914) 256-6351

May 28, 1995

Dean Phillips
Manager
Home Menu Cafe
946 W. 33rd Street
Chicago, IL 60608

Dear Mr. Phillips:

I would like to thank you for taking the time to speak with me. I really enjoyed talking to you about your restaurant and the cook position.

As we discussed, I have four years' experience as a cook in a busy restaurant, and I work well with other people. I am also a fast learner, so I can learn your menu very easily.

I am very interested in working in your restaurant. I look forward to hearing from you soon.

Sincerely,

Gloria Alonso

Gloria Alonso

Now, write your own thank-you letter to John Muraki.

He is the human resources director at American Networks. His address is 2020 4th Street, San Rafael, California 94901. You had an interview with him today for your short-term goal.

Your name, address, and telephone number	_____ _____ _____ _____
Today's date	_____
Interviewer's name and title	_____ _____
Company name and address	_____ _____

Mr./Ms. + last name

Thank the interviewer. Say you enjoyed talking to him/her.

Review your experience, work skills, or personal qualities.

Dear _____:

I would like to thank you for taking the time to speak with me. I really enjoyed talking to you about _____.

As we discussed, _____

_____

_____

_____

I am very interested in working in your _____. I look forward to hearing from you soon.

Sincerely,

Sign your name.   _____

Type your name.   _____

FOLLOW-UP: Telephone Call

Sometimes you need to make a telephone call after an interview. You
should ask the interviewer, "Should I contact you or will you contact me?"
at the end of an interview. When the interviewer says, "You can contact
me," you need to call him or her.

HOW TO MAKE A FOLLOW-UP TELEPHONE CALL

When you call and talk to the interviewer, you should do these things:

- Introduce yourself.
- Say why you are calling.
- Tell the interviewer that you are still interested in the job.
- Ask the interviewer if he or she has made a decision.

46 TEAM WORK

Complete the applicant's part of the conversation, using the sentences in
the box. Use your name and your short-term job goal. Then form groups
of three and practice the conversation.

> I'm still very interested in the job.
> Okay. Thank you very much.
> I had an interview for the job as a (your short-term goal).
> ✓ Could I speak to Terri Massin, please?
> Have you made a decision about the position?
> Tuesday morning?

Receptionist: May I help you?

Applicant: Yes. My name is _____ (your name) _____.
Could I speak to Terri Massin, please?

Receptionist: One moment, please.

Interviewer: Terri Massin speaking.

Applicant: Hello, Ms. Massin. This is _____ (your name) _____.
_____

Interviewer: Oh, yes. Thanks for calling. What can I do for you?

Applicant: _____

Interviewer: That's good. I'm glad you're still interested. I enjoyed talking to you.

Applicant: _____

Interviewer: No, I haven't made a decision. Could you call back next
Tuesday morning?

Applicant: _____

Interviewer: That's right.

Applicant: _____

Interviewer: You're welcome. Goodbye.

47 APPLY YOURSELF

Contact three companies that might have job openings for you. Apply for a job in each company. Fill out job applications, give managers your cover letter and resume, or send managers your cover letter and resume. Then fill in the chart below.

	Company #1	Company #2	Company #3
Date you applied for the job			
How you applied for the job			
Name of company			
Address of company			
Telephone number of company			
Manager's name			
Follow-up information			

48 TEAM WORK

Work in small groups. Discuss the following questions about what you did in Exercise 47.

1. What job(s) did you apply for?

2. How did you apply at each company?

3. Did you talk to the managers? If so, what did each manager say?

4. What do you need to do next?

WHAT DO YOU THINK NOW?

Discuss these questions with your classmates.

1. How can you sell yourself at a job interview?

2. What should you talk about when an interviewer asks you about your strengths?

3. What are some things you should remember when you talk about your weaknesses?

4. What should you talk about when an interviewer asks you about your goals?

5. How should you follow up after a job interview?

49 REVIEW: Board Game

Listen to your teacher's instructions. Then play the game.

WINNER

What part of your work needs the most improvement? ¿

Talk about good body language. ☒

What shifts can you work? ¿

Talk about the information you need to know before you go to an interview. ☒

What were your major responsibilities in your last job? ¿

Give an example of enthusiasm. ☒

Talk about two things you should bring to an interview. ☒

Why should I hire you? ¿

Tell me about yourself. ¿

Talk about mistakes you can make when you talk about weaknesses. ☒

Give a concrete example of one of your strengths. ☒

Talk about three things you should not do at an interview. ☒

What kind of salary are you looking for? ¿

What are your best work abilities and best qualities? ¿

What would you like to be doing in three to five years? ¿

Give an example of active listening. ☒

You are an employer. Talk about the kind of applicant you are looking for. ☒

Talk about how to sell yourself. ☒

What kind of experience do you have that will help you in this job? ¿

Talk about a good thank-you letter. ☒

START
START

You are at a job interview. Introduce yourself to the receptionist. ☒

Do you want to work part-time or full-time? ¿

APPENDIXES
Information Gap Exercises

Unit 1, 30 PAIR WORK

INFORMATION GAP: Student B, look at this page. Student A, look at page 25.

You and your partner will read a story about Yolanda's job search. This story has two parts.

1. Read Part B of the story to yourself. Look only at this page.

2. Listen to your partner tell you Part A of the story, and answer his or her questions.

3. Then tell your story to your partner in your own words.

4. Ask your partner the questions about the story.

PART B: YOLANDA'S JOB SEARCH

Yolanda worked as a waitress for a year. She liked to work with people, but she did not want to work in a restaurant all her life. She wanted to work with children.

Yolanda started to network. She told her co-workers and friends that she wanted a new job. One day her co-worker said, "I have good news! My friend, Julie Kapp, needs a child care worker. Julie has two children, and she works every day."

Yolanda called Ms. Kapp. She sent Ms. Kapp her resume. Then she went to Ms. Kapp's house for an interview. Yolanda was nervous, but very friendly. Ms. Kapp liked her, and Yolanda got the job.

Yolanda has worked for Ms. Kapp for two years. She likes her job as a child care worker because she likes to organize games and teach children. She is a hard worker, and she is very patient. Now she is studying at night because she wants to be a teacher's assistant. In the future, Yolanda hopes to be a teacher again.

1. How long did Yolanda work at her first job in the United States?

2. How did she find her next job?

3. What is her job now? Does she like it?

4. What are some of Yolanda's job duties now?

5. What is Yolanda doing at night?

6. What does Yolanda want to do in the future?

7. What are Yolanda's transferable skills for her next job goal?

Unit 2, 7 ROLE PLAYS

INFORMATION GAP: Student B, look at this page. Student A, look at page 32.

Work with a partner. Read the first situation. Then create a conversation. When you finish, read the second situation. Create another conversation.

1. You are a receptionist in a business. Student A is looking for a job. Your manager, Lucia Ramirez, is out now. She will be in today at 4:00 P.M.

2. You are looking for a job as (your job goal). You walk into a business and talk to the receptionist. Introduce yourself and say that you are looking for a job. If the manager isn't there, ask for an application, ask when the manager will be in, and ask for the manager's name.

Unit 2, 17 ROLE PLAYS

INFORMATION GAP: Student B, look at this page. Student A, look at page 40.

Work with a partner. Read the first situation. Then create a conversation. When you finish, read the second situation. Create another conversation.

1. Student B, you are the manager of a business. Student A is a job applicant. You have a job opening in your business. Tell the applicant about the job.

    *   The job begins _____(day)_____.

    *   The hours are _____ to _____.

2. Student B, you are a job applicant. Student A is the manager of a business. You are looking for a job as (your job goal). You walked into the company to ask if there are any job openings.

    Don't forget to:

    *   Tell the manager about your skills, qualities, or experience.

    *   Ask for an application or to leave a resume.

    *   Ask if there will be any openings in the future.

Unit 2, 34 ROLE PLAYS

INFORMATION GAP: Student B, look at this page. Student A, look at page 56.

Work with a partner. Read the first situation. Then create a conversation. When you finish, read the second situation. Create another conversation.

1. Student B, you are Student A's friend. Student A is looking for a job and asks you for help. Your manager, (name), is looking for a new employee. Tell Student A to call your manager. Tell Student A that your manager's telephone number is _____ .

2. Student B, you are looking for a job as (your job goal). You are networking with Student A. Student A is your neighbor. Ask your neighbor to help you.

Unit 2, 38 ROLE PLAYS

INFORMATION GAP: Student B, look at this page. Student A, look at page 58.

Work with a partner. Read the first situation. Then create a conversation. When you finish, read the second situation. Create another conversation.

1. Student B, you do not know Student A. Student A is looking for a job. Student A calls you. Tell Student A that you don't know about any jobs now. Tell Student A to call you back in two weeks.

2. Student B, you are looking for a job as (your job goal). A few days ago, you networked with your neighbor, and your neighbor told you to call Student A. You do not know Student A. Call Student A and network.

Unit 2, 42 REVIEW: Cooperative Crossword Puzzle

INFORMATION GAP: Student B, look at this page. Student A , look at page 62.

There are two different clues for each word. Read your clue to your partner. Listen to your partner's clue. Then choose the correct word from the list. Write it in the spaces.

EXAMPLE: Student A: #1 Down. "You can send your resume with this machine."

Student B: #1 Down. "This machine has a number like a telephone number."

ABBREVIATION
ANNOUNCEMENTS
APPLICATION
BODY LANGUAGE
DUTIES
EXPERIENCE
✔ FAX
HELP WANTED
MANAGER
NETWORKING
OPENINGS
PREFERRED
RESUME
WANT ADS
WALK IN

ACROSS CLUES

2. This is good when you smile and shake hands firmly.
6. Exp., exper.
8. You can find these at an employment agency.
10. A paper you fill out when you are looking for a job.
11. This means "not required."
12. Classified ads, employment opportunities.
14. When you walk in, you ask the manager, "Do you have any _____?"
15. This is a typed document about your work history.

DOWN CLUES

1. This machine has a number like a telephone number.
3. A short way to write words in want ads.
4. Look for this heading in the newspaper when you need a job.
5. You want to talk to this person when you walk in.
7. Telling your friends and other people that you are looking for a job.
9. You can do this at a store or a restaurant.
13. An example is, "Responsible for TV and radio repair."

⌒ Unit 3, 1 LISTENING

Message #1:   Hello. You've reached the Acme Company. Nobody can answer the phone right now. Our business hours are Monday to Friday from 8:00 A.M. to 5:00 P.M. Please call back during regular office hours. Thank you very much.

Message #2:   Hello. Thank you for calling Metropolitan Bank. Nobody can take your call right now. Please leave a message with your name and telephone number. We'll return your call as soon as possible. Thank you.

Message #3:   Hi. This is Juanita Gomez. I'm either away from my desk or on the phone. Please leave a message after the beep. I'll call you back as soon as I can. If you'd like to be connected with the receptionist, please press zero now, and someone will be right with you.

Message #4:   You've reached Grand Star. All of our lines are currently busy. Please hold, and your call will be answered shortly.

Unit 3, 29 ROLE PLAYS

INFORMATION GAP: Student B, look at this page. Student A, look at page 82.

Work with a partner. Read the first situation. Then create a conversation. When you finish, read the second situation. Create another conversation.

1. Student B, you are a job applicant. Student A is a receptionist. You are looking for a job as (your job goal). You call Projects International. Introduce yourself. Remember to ask for the manager's name and a good time to call back. Leave a good message. Ask questions if you do not understand. Write down all important information.

    Notes: Manager's name: _____

    When to call back: _____

2. Student B, you are the receptionist at the Fuller Company. Student A is a job applicant. The personnel manager, Sonia Chung, is not in the office. She will be available at 2:30 this afternoon. Take a message. Use the message form below. Remember to write down the name, the telephone number, and the job.

P H O N E M E M O	TO		DATE	TIME	AM PM
	FROM		PHONE NO.		
	M E S S A G E				

Unit 4, 19 PAIR WORK

INFORMATION GAP: Student B, look at this page. Student A, look at page 99.

1. Talk to your partner (Student A). Read each sentence to your partner. Your partner will write down the important information you say. Answer your partner's questions. When you finish, check your partner's answers.

   a. Can you come to an interview on Thursday, January 13th, at 1:00?

   b. The address is 1676 Burton St.

   c. The cross streets are Clay and Spring.

   d. The ZIP code is 59802.

   e. My name is Linda Louie.

2. Talk to your partner (Student A). Your partner will read some sentences. Write the important information (names, addresses, dates, and times) you hear. Repeat the information your partner tells you. Ask questions when you do not understand. Check the spelling of names and streets. When you finish, check your answers with your partner.

   f. _____

   g. _____

   h. _____

   i. _____

   j. _____

Unit 4, 23 ROLE PLAYS

INFORMATION GAP: Student B, look at this page. Student A, look at page 102.

Work with a partner. Read the first situation. Then create a conversation. When you finish, read the second situation. Create another conversation.

1. Student B, you are a job applicant. You call Student A, a manager. Introduce yourself. Then tell the manager a little more about your experience or your transferable skills. Write the information the manager tells you. Repeat all of the information. Ask questions when you don't understand.

    Notes: _____

    _____

    _____

2. Student B, you are a manager. Student A calls you about a job. Ask Student A to tell you more about his or her experience. Then ask him or her to send you a resume. Use this information:

Manager's name:	Pat Herrera
Street address:	689 Gainesville Street
City and state:	Houston, Texas
ZIP code:	77015

⌢ Unit 5, 1 LISTENING

Roger: I look for complete applications. It's important to answer all the questions. For example, if someone doesn't fill out dates and numbers, or an address, I think that person is not good with details, and I will not hire that person. I need workers who will complete every detail of the job and who know how to follow instructions.

Lilya: Sometimes I get applications that I can't read because of the handwriting. People write in so many different ways, and some people's handwriting is impossible to read! I think job applicants should always print or type their applications. And please use a pen, not a pencil. The information is really important. After all, I can't call an applicant if I can't read the name.

Dean: I agree with Lilya. I think people should print. But I want to add that they should print *neatly* and *clearly*. People need to be careful when they fill out their applications. I mean, they shouldn't cross out words, and I really don't like spelling mistakes. If someone makes a mistake, then that person should ask for a new application or correct the mistakes very, *very* carefully.

Unit 6, 22 REVIEW: Cooperative Crossword Puzzle

INFORMATION GAP: Student B, look at this page. Student A, look at page 156.

There are two different clues for each word. Read your clue to your partner. Listen to your partner's clue. Then choose the correct word from the list. Write it in the spaces.

EXAMPLE: Student A: #1 Down. "You can get this document when you finish technical school."

Student B: #1 Down. "You get this when you study auto repair or cosmetology."

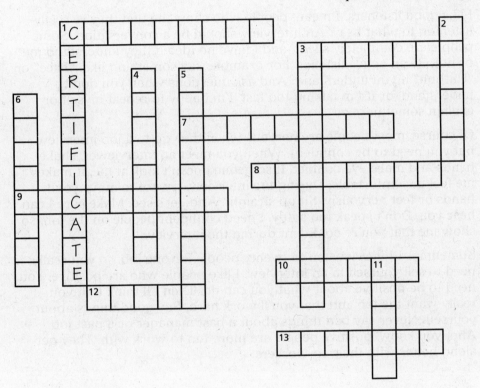

✔ CERTIFICATE
COLLEGE
COVER LETTER
CURRENTLY
DEGREE
DIPLOMA
GRADUATE
MAJOR
PRINTING
REFERENCE
RELATIVE
RESUME
SHIFT
U.S. CITIZEN
WORK PERMIT

DOWN CLUES

1. You can get this when you study auto repair or cosmetology.
2. Examples are: A.A., B.S., M.S., Ph.D.
3. You send this with your resume.
4. Do not use this for your signature.
5. If you are under 18, you can work when you have this document.
6. People in the United States usually do this in May or June.
11. Your most important subject in college.

ACROSS CLUES

1. Another way to say "presently."
3. You must complete this before you go to graduate school.
7. Managers call this person to find out about you.
8. Examples are: mother, brother, cousin.
9. A person born in the United States.
10. A one-page document about your skills and experience.
12. Examples are: day, swing, evening.
13. You get this document when you finish twelve grades.

⌒ Unit 7, 3 LISTENING

1. I don't really want to hear about your personal problems or your life in general. I mean, what's happening with your husband, your wife, or your family—any of that. I'm an interviewer, not a friend. This is a business conversation. I just want to know if you're the best person for the job. I want to hear about your past jobs, your skills, and your qualities.

2. You need to answer questions completely. Give examples. If someone tells me she worked as a salesperson, I want to know what she did. Did she collect money? Did she put away clothes? Did she talk to customers? If someone says he is flexible, I want more information. Can he work any schedule? Can he change duties easily? When I'm deciding who to hire, I remember the applicants who gave examples.

3. I like good listeners. I mean, people who show me that they're really listening to what I say. An interview should be a conversation. Some people are completely silent, and I have no idea if they understand me or not. Be an active listener. For example, say something like, "I see" or "Uh-huh" if you understand. And ask questions when you don't understand, or if I'm talking too fast. I'm happy to repeat myself or explain something.

4. Of course, most people are nervous when they go to a job interview, but you need to be confident. When you meet an interviewer, shake hands and make eye contact. If someone doesn't look at me, it makes me feel uncomfortable. During the interview, try not to move your hands or feet nervously. Sit up straight. And, let's see. Make sure I can hear you. Don't speak too softly. I need confident people on the job, so show me that you're confident during the interview.

5. Sometimes I interview ten to twenty people for one job, so you really need to sell yourself in an interview. I like people who are positive. You need to be positive about what you can do. Then I'll think that you really want the job and that you'll work hard. Say good things about yourself. Never say bad things about a past manager or a past job. And, you know, positive people are more fun to work with. They get along better with their co-workers.

⌒ Unit 7, 20 ROLE PLAYS

INFORMATION GAP: Student B, look at this page. Student A, look at page 174.

Work with a partner. Read the first situation. Then create a conversation. When you finish, read the second situation. Create another conversation. Applicants, remember to be enthusiastic, use active listening, and use good body language.

1. You are a job applicant at an interview. Answer the interviewer's questions. Ask questions when you don't understand. Repeat and write down the information the interviewer tells you.

   Notes: _____

   _____

   _____

   _____

2. You are an interviewer. You are interviewing Student A. Ask, "What job are you applying for?" Ask basic interview questions. For example, "What days can you work?" If you do not remember basic interview questions, look at page 165. Tell the applicant this information about the job:

Part-time	12:00 P.M to 6:00 P.M.
Permanent	$7.25 an hour
Thursday through Sunday	Starts on Thursday, September 21st

Alphabet

PRINT

A a B b C c D d E e F f G g H h I i

J j K k L l M m N n O o P p Q q

R r S s T t U u V v W w X x Y y Z z

SCRIPT

Tapescript

UNIT 1, EXERCISE 1, page 2

Alex: Hi, Regina. How are you doing?

Regina: Good. How about you?

Alex: Well, I'm okay, but I really need a job and I don't know what to do. I've never looked for a job in this country.

Regina: Hum. . . Well, first you need to think about your personal qualities. What kind of person are you? Do you like to work with people? Do you learn quickly?

Alex: Oh yes, I'm very friendly. I work well with people, and I'm a fast learner.

Regina: Okay. What are your work skills?

Alex: What do you mean?

Regina: Well, can you use a computer? Can you cook? Can you help sick people?

Alex: I can help sick people.

Regina: Oh, really. What was your last job?

Alex: I was a nurse.

Regina: And what do you want to do here?

Alex: I want to be a nurse here, too.

Regina: Well, that's a good long-term goal. Maybe you can work as a nurse in a few years.

Alex: A few years? But I need a job now!

Regina: So, you need a short-term job goal. For example, you can be a home health aide now.

Alex: What's that?

Regina: You help sick people in their homes, maybe a very old person.

Alex: Oh, yeah. I can do that.

Regina: And then you can study at night to become a nurse.

Alex: Okay, but how can I start?

Regina: Well, your goals are good, but now you need to write down all your work skills and personal qualities.

Alex: Why?

Regina: Because you need to say good things about yourself to managers. Managers need to know that you are the best person for the job.

Alex: Okay.

Regina: And then you need to write your resume.

Alex: A resume?

Regina: Yes. You need to write *one page* about your job goal, your skills and personal qualities, and your education and past jobs.

Alex: That's a lot!

Regina: Don't worry. I'll help you.

UNIT 1, EXERCISE 8, page 6

1. I am a sales clerk. I'm energetic. I'm good with numbers.
2. I am a teacher's assistant. I work well with people. I'm patient.
3. I am an office clerk. I'm organized. I'm flexible.
4. I am a baggage porter. I'm a hard worker. I'm strong.
5. I am a cook. I'm efficient. I work well under pressure.
6. I am a musician. I'm creative. I'm a fast learner.
7. I am a painter. I'm careful with details. I'm good with my hands.
8. I am a computer technician. I'm a good problem solver. I'm reliable.

UNIT 1, EXERCISES 13 & 14, pages 10 & 11

1. Interviewer: Hi. My name is Fulani Washington. I'm a student at Longshore Community College, and I'm interviewing people about their jobs. Could I ask you a few questions?

   Pedro: Sure.

   Interviewer: What's your name?

   Pedro: Pedro Santos.

   Interviewer: What kind of work did you do?

   Pedro: I was a gardener.

   Interviewer: Oh, interesting. What were your job duties?

   Pedro: Well, I planted grass and flowers. I really love wildflowers. I cared for plants and trees, and I really like to grow things.

   Interviewer: I can see that. Well, thanks a lot, Pedro.

   Pedro: You're welcome. Goodbye.

   Interviewer: Goodbye.

2. Interviewer: Hi. My name is Fulani Washington. I'm a student at Longshore Community College, and I'm interviewing people about their jobs. Could I ask you a few questions, please?

   Lee: Sure.

   Interviewer: What's your name?

   Lee: Lee Johnson.

   Interviewer: And what kind of work did you do?

   Lee: I was a lab assistant in a small hospital.

   Interviewer: Uh-huh. How was that?

   Lee: It was a great job!

   Interviewer: Good. What were your job duties?

   Lee: I did lab tests, for example, blood tests, and I cleaned and organized lab equipment. I really loved working in a hospital.

   Interviewer: Well, I hope you find a job in a hospital again soon!

   Lee: Me, too.

3. Interviewer: Hi. My name is Fulani Washington. I'm a student at Longshore Community College, and I'm interviewing people about their jobs. Could I ask you a few questions, please?

   Jade: Sure.

   Interviewer: What's your name?

   Jade: Jade Chen.

   Interviewer: Nice to meet you, Jade. And, what was your last job?

   Jade: I was a cashier.

   Interviewer: A cashier. Did you like it?

   Jade: Yes, I liked it a lot.

   Interviewer: What were your duties?

   Jade: Well, I worked in a really nice store. I used a cash register. It was just like a computer, but easier to use. And I collected cash, checks, and charge payments from the customers.

   Interviewer: It sounds like it was a lot of fun. Well, it was nice talking to you. Thanks a lot.

   Jade: You're welcome. Goodbye.

   Interviewer: Goodbye.

UNIT 1, EXERCISES 22 & 23, pages 20 & 21

Yolanda: Hi, Aree.

Aree: Hi, Yolanda. How's the job search going?

Yolanda: Oh, it's really hard. You know I was a teacher in my country, and I want to be a teacher here, too. But I can't.

Aree: Why not?

Yolanda: Because I don't have a teaching certificate.

Aree: Well, you need a short-term goal, and you need to think about your transferable skills.

Yolanda: Transferable skills? What are those?

Aree: Those are personal qualities and work skills from your old job that you can use in your new job.

Yolanda: Oh?

Aree: I'll explain. What do you like to do?

Yolanda: I really like to work with people. As a teacher, I worked with people every day.

Aree: And I bet you were a good teacher. You're so energetic and you're patient, too.

Yolanda: Well, thank you. I think I'm also very organized.

Aree: The point is that those are transferable skills. You can use those qualities in a job as a waitress. I think that's a great short-term goal for you. A waitress works with people, and a waitress needs to be energetic because restaurants get very busy.

Yolanda: Oh, I see! And as a teacher, I needed to be very organized to prepare my lesson plans. A waitress needs be organized, too, because she has many food orders.

Aree: That's it!

Yolanda: But what about my work skills? Are those transferable skills too?

Aree: Sure, sometimes. Tell me your work skills.

Yolanda: Well, I know how to teach classes, but that's not a transferable skill.

Aree: Not for a waitress. What else can you do?

Yolanda: I can answer questions from students and parents.

Aree: That's a good one. A waitress needs to answer customers' questions.

Yolanda: And I know how to talk to students and help them with their schoolwork. I guess a waitress helps customers decide what to eat.

Aree: Right! What about other things you do well, besides teaching? Life skills can also be transferable skills.

Yolanda: Let me think. I'm good at fixing things in my house. I'm really good with my hands.

Aree: That's not very important for a waitress.

Yolanda: No, it isn't. Hum. What else? I'm really good at math. I make a budget every month. I know how much money I have, and I never spend too much.

Aree: So you're good with numbers. That's a great skill for a waitress!

UNIT 1, EXERCISE 29, page 24

May: Hi, Alex. I haven't seen you in a long time. How are you doing?

Alex: Great! I just got a new job!

May: That's wonderful. What are you doing?

Alex: I'm working as a baggage porter.

May: Oh. How did you find out about the job?

Alex: Well, I saw a "Help Wanted" sign in the window of a small hotel downtown. I walked in, introduced myself, and asked to speak to the manager.

May: Uh-huh.

Alex: The woman at the front desk asked me to fill out an application first.

May: And did you talk to the manager? Did you have an interview?

Alex: Well, I did talk to the manager, but my interview was really short. The manager asked me a few questions and then told me to come to work on Saturday.

May: You must be happy.

Alex: Yes. Well, I heard you have a new job, too. How is it?

May: I really like it. I'm working as a photo lab assistant. I looked for a *long* time before I found this job.

Alex: Oh, where did you look?

May: I read the want ads in the newspaper, but I only found two job openings. I sent my resume to one company, but I didn't get the job.

Alex: So, how did you finally find your job?

May: I networked.

Alex: Really?

May: Yeah. I told my neighbor I was looking for a job, and her friend needed a photo lab assistant. I called him on the telephone.

Alex: Uh-huh.

May: I went in for an interview, and he asked me a lot of

questions. I was really nervous. But he called me a few days later and told me I got the job.

Alex: That's really great!

UNIT 2, EXERCISE 1, page 28

Receptionist: Good morning.

Applicant: Hello. My name is Alicia Sanchez. I'm interested in a job in this hotel. Could I talk to the manager, please?

Receptionist: I'm sorry. He isn't here right now. Can I help you?

Applicant: Yes. I'm interested in a job as a housekeeper.

Receptionist: I'm sorry. We don't have any openings right now.

Applicant: Could I fill out an application anyway, please?

Receptionist: Sure. Here you are.

Applicant: Thanks. May I have the manager's name, please?

Receptionist: Sure. His name is Jerry Brown.

Applicant: Jerry Brown?

Receptionist: Right.

Applicant: Could you tell me when the manager will be in, please?

Receptionist: He'll be in this afternoon.

Applicant: Okay. I'll come back this afternoon. Thank you very much.

Receptionist: No problem.

Applicant: Goodbye.

Receptionist: Goodbye.

UNIT 2, EXERCISES 3 & 4, pages 29 & 30

1. Receptionist: Good morning.

   Applicant: Hello. My name is Alicia Sanchez. I'm interested in a job in this hotel. Could I talk to the manager, please?

   Receptionist: I'm sorry. He isn't here right now. Can I help you?

   Applicant: Yes. I'm interested in a job as a housekeeper.

   Receptionist: I'm sorry. We don't have any openings right now.

   Applicant: Could I fill out an application anyway, please?

   Receptionist: Sure. Here you are.

   Applicant: Thanks. May I have the manager's name, please?

   Receptionist: Sure. His name is Jerry Brown.

   Applicant: Jerry Brown?

   Receptionist: Right.

   Applicant: Could you tell me when the manager will be in, please?

   Receptionist: He'll be in this afternoon.

   Applicant: Okay. I'll come back this afternoon. Thank you very much.

   Receptionist: No problem.

   Applicant: Goodbye.

   Receptionist: Goodbye.

2. Receptionist: Hello. May I help you?

   Applicant: My name is Jamie Francisco, and . . . I'm looking for a job as a taxi driver.

   Receptionist: Sorry, we don't have any jobs right now.

   Applicant: Okay. Could you tell me the manager's name, please?

   Receptionist: Sure. Her name is Pat Zody.

   Applicant: Pat Zody. Thank you very much.

   Receptionist: You're welcome. Goodbye.

   Applicant: Goodbye.

3. Receptionist: Good afternoon. May I help you?

   Applicant: Good afternoon. I'm Rosa Borik. I saw your "Help Wanted" sign in the window and I'm looking for a job. May I speak to the person who does the hiring, please?

   Receptionist: I'm afraid the manager isn't in right now.

Applicant:	Excuse me?
Receptionist:	The manager isn't here.
Applicant:	Oh, I see. May I have an application, please?
Receptionist:	Sure.
Applicant:	Could you tell me when the manager will be available, please?
Receptionist:	She'll be in at 3:00 today.
Applicant:	Okay. I'll come back at 3:00. Thank you for your help.
Receptionist:	You're welcome.
Applicant:	Goodbye.
Receptionist:	Goodbye.

UNIT 2, EXERCISE 8, page 33

Receptionist:	Hi.
Applicant:	Hello. My name is Maw Win, and I'm interested in a job as a cook. Could I speak to the manager, please?
Receptionist:	I'll see if she's here.
Manager:	Hello. Can I help you?
Applicant:	Yes. My name is Maw Win, and I'm interested in a job as a cook in your restaurant.
Manager:	Well, we have a job opening now.
Applicant:	Could you say that again, please?
Manager:	We need a cook now.
Applicant:	Great!
Manager:	Do you have any experience as a cook?
Applicant:	Yes. I worked as a cook for six months at The Corner Cafe. I'm very efficient and friendly. I would really like to work in your restaurant.
Manager:	That's good.
Applicant:	May I have an application, please?
Manager:	Of course. Here you are.
Applicant:	Could you tell me when the job starts, please?
Manager:	It starts next Wednesday.
Applicant:	Next Wednesday. Could you tell me the hours?
Manager:	4:00 P.M. to 12:00 A.M., Wednesday through Sunday.
Applicant:	Four to twelve, Wednesday through Sunday. That sounds great. And is this a full-time or a part-time job?
Manager:	It's full-time, forty hours a week.
Applicant:	That's what I'm looking for, a full-time job.
Manager:	Well, I'll look at your application and call you in a few days.
Applicant:	Thanks a lot.
Manager:	You're welcome.
Applicant:	Goodbye.
Manager:	Goodbye.

UNIT 2, EXERCISES 10 & 11, page 35

1.
Manager:	Hello. Can I help you?
Applicant:	Yes. My name is Sang Lao, and I'm interested in a job as a salesperson. I'm flexible and I work well with others. I know how to collect money and help customers. I have one year's experience at Macy's. I'd really like to work in this store.
Manager:	I'm afraid we don't have any openings now.
Applicant:	May I have an application anyway, please?
Manager:	Sure. Here you are.
Applicant:	Thanks. May I leave a resume, please?
Manager:	Sure. This looks like a nice resume!
Applicant:	Thank you. Will you have any openings in the future?
Manager:	Well, maybe in a few months.
Applicant:	Okay. I'll call you in a few months. Thank you very much.
Manager:	You're welcome.
Applicant:	Goodbye.
Manager:	Goodbye.

2.
Manager:	Hello, Mr. Kumar. May I help you?
Applicant:	Yes, I really need a job. I want to be an office clerk. I'm organized, and I know how to type.
Manager:	I'm sorry. We don't have any openings now.
Applicant:	Well, could I leave my resume anyway, please?
Manager:	Sure, Mr. Kumar.
Applicant:	Will there be any work here later on?
Manager	I'm not sure. Why don't you call me in a month?
Applicant:	Okay. Thank you.
Manger:	You're welcome. Goodbye.
Applicant:	Goodbye.

3.
Manager:	Hello. Can I help you?
Applicant:	Yes. My name is Maw Win, and I'm interested in a job as a cook in your restaurant.
Manager:	Well, we have a job opening now.
Applicant:	Could you say that again, please?
Manager:	We need a cook now.
Applicant:	Great!
Manager:	Do you have any experience as a cook?
Applicant:	Yes. I worked at The Corner Cafe for six months as a cook. I'm very efficient and friendly. I would really like to work in your restaurant.
Manager:	That's good.
Applicant:	Could I fill out an application, please?
Manager:	Of course. Here you are.
Applicant:	Could you tell me the working hours, please?
Manager:	4:00 P.M. to 12:00 A.M., Wednesday through Sunday.
Applicant:	That sounds fine. Could you tell me when the job starts, please?
Manager:	It starts next Wednesday.
Applicant:	And is this a full-time or a part-time job?
Manager:	It's full-time, forty hours a week.
Applicant:	That's what I'm looking for, a full-time job.
Manager:	Well, I'll look at your application and call you in a few days.
Applicant:	Thanks a lot.
Manager:	You're welcome.
Applicant:	Goodbye.
Manager:	Goodbye.

UNIT 2, EXERCISE 30, page 52

1.
Jessica:	Hi, Kareem.
Kareem:	Hi, Jessica. Nice day to wash the car. I should wash mine, too!
Jessica:	Yeah, it seems like all our neighbors are washing their cars today.
Kareem:	So, how have you been?
Jessica:	Good. How about you?
Kareem:	Okay, I guess, but I'm looking for a job.
Jessica:	Really? What kind of job are you looking for?
Kareem:	A job as an office clerk. Do you know where I could look?
Jessica:	Well, you could talk to my friend, Bob. He works in a big company downtown. Let me give you his number.
Kareem:	Oh, thanks a lot.

2.
Jamal:	Hello?
Kareem:	Hello, Jamal? This is Kareem Halaj. How are you?
Jamal:	Oh, Kareem. I'm fine. And you?
Kareem:	Pretty good. How's everything at the office?
Jamal:	The same as when you worked here. Nothing has changed.
Kareem:	Well, I miss the office.
Jamal:	We miss you, too. So, have you found a new job yet?
Kareem:	No, I haven't found anything yet. I'm interested in working as an office clerk, and I was wondering if you could help me.

Jamal: Certainly. How can I help?
Kareem: Well, if you find out about any jobs, could you call me?
Jamal: I'd be happy to, Kareem.
Kareem: May I send you my resume?
Jamal: Yes, that's a good idea.
Kareem: Thank you very much for your help, Jamal.
Jamal: It's my pleasure.

3. Daryl: That was a great soccer game, Kareem!
Kareem: Yeah. You played really well, Daryl.
Daryl: So did you! Are you coming to the game tomorrow afternoon?
Kareem: Well, I'm not sure. I'm looking for a job, and I'm very busy.
Daryl: Oh, I didn't know you were looking for a job.
Kareem: Yes, I'm looking for a job as an office clerk. Could you help me?
Daryl: Maybe. What can I do?
Kareem: Well, if you hear of any jobs, could you call me?
Daryl: Sure.
Kareem: Do you know anyone I could talk to?
Daryl: Well, I'll talk to a few people I know. . . and . . . why don't you call me next week.
Kareem: Great. Could I give you my resume?
Daryl: That would be helpful.
Kareem: Thanks a lot. Well, I'll talk to you next week.

4. Kareem: Uncle Amir. Wonderful barbecue. The food is great!
Amir: I'm glad you like it. It's so nice to be with family and friends.
Kareem: I think so, too. You know, Uncle Amir, I'm looking for a job.
Amir: Yes?
Kareem: Could you help me?
Amir: Sure, let me think. Well, one of my friends is here. She works for a construction company. Let me introduce you to her.

Amir: Kareem, I'd like to introduce my friend, Hiromi. Hiromi, this is my nephew, Kareem.
Hiromi: Nice to meet you, Kareem.
Kareem: Nice to meet you, too.
Amir: Hiromi works for the Miyako Construction Company.
Kareem: Oh, that's interesting.
Hiromi: And what do you do, Kareem?
Kareem: Well, right now I'm looking for a job as an office clerk.
Hiromi: Oh, really. I'll talk to the other people in my office.
Kareem: If you hear of any jobs, could you call me?
Hiromi: Of course.
Kareem: And could I give my resume to you?
Hiromi: Why don't you send it to me.
Kareem: Okay. Thank you very much.

5. Ms. Turner: Hello, Mr. Halaj.
Kareem: Hello, Ms. Turner.
Ms. Turner: Come on in. Let me find your papers. You know, we have to fill out so many papers for the government. I'm sorry.
Kareem: Oh, that's okay.
Ms. Turner: How is your job search going?
Kareem: Okay, I guess.
Ms. Turner: Did you do any networking?
Kareem: Yes, I talked to my neighbor, and I talked to my past co-worker. Then, oh, I met a woman at my uncle's barbecue. I'm going to send my resume to her. And, let's see. I talked to my soccer teammate.
Ms. Turner: Wow! You really know how to network, don't you?
Kareem: Yes, I do. I was wondering if you could help me, too.

Ms. Turner: Yes, I think I can. Why don't you fill out these forms. Let's see . . .
Kareem: Do you know where I could look?
Ms. Turner: Yes, I do know one company. . .

UNIT 2, EXERCISE 32, page 54

1. Kareem: So, how have you been?
Jessica: Good. How about you?
Kareem: Okay, I guess, but I'm looking for a job.
Jessica: Really? What kind of job are you looking for?
Kareem: A job as an office clerk. Do you know where I could look?
Jessica: Well, you could talk to my friend, Bob. He works in a big company downtown. Let me give you his number.
Kareem: Oh, thanks a lot.

2. Jamal: Hello?
Kareem: Hello, Jamal? This is Kareem Halaj. How are you?
Jamal: Oh, Kareem. I'm fine. And you?
Kareem: Pretty good.
Jamal: So, have you found a new job yet?
Kareem: No, I haven't found anything yet. You know, I'm interested in working as an office clerk, and I was wondering if you could help me.
Jamal: Certainly. How can I help?
Kareem: Well, if you find out about any jobs, could you call me?
Jamal: I'd be happy to, Kareem.
Kareem: May I send you my resume?
Jamal: Yes, that's a good idea.
Kareem: Thank you very much for your help, Jamal.
Jamal: It's my pleasure.

3. Daryl: Are you coming to the game tomorrow afternoon?
Kareem: Well, I'm not sure. I'm looking for a job, and I'm very busy.
Daryl: Oh, I didn't know you were looking for a job.
Kareem: Yes, I'm looking for a job as an office clerk. Could you help me?
Daryl: Maybe. What can I do?
Kareem: Well, if you hear of any jobs, could you call me?
Daryl: Sure.
Kareem: Do you know anyone I could talk to?
Daryl: Well, I'll talk to a few people I know. . . and . . . why don't you call me next week.
Kareem: Great. Could I give you my resume?
Daryl: That would be helpful.
Kareem: Thanks a lot. Well, I'll talk to you next week.

UNIT 2, EXERCISE 36, page 57

Sonia: Hi. My name is Sonia Chang. My friend, Mario Martinez, told me to call you.
Anna: Oh, Mario. How is he?
Sonia: Good. I'm calling because I'm looking for a job as a waitress.
Anna: Uh-huh.
Sonia: He said that you might have some job openings in your restaurant.
Anna: Well, actually, I think we need a waitress now. Could you call back tomorrow?
Sonia: Sure. Thanks a lot.
Anna: You're welcome. Goodbye.
Sonia: Goodbye.

UNIT 3, EXERCISE 1, page 64

1. Hello. You've reached the Acme Company. Nobody can answer the phone right now. Our business hours are Monday to Friday from 8:00 A.M. to 5:00 P.M. Please call back during regular office hours. Thank you very much.

2. Hello. Thank you for calling Metropolitan Bank. Nobody can take your call right now. Please leave a message with your name and telephone number. We'll return your call as soon as possible. Thank you.

3. Hi. This is Juanita Gomez. I'm either away from my desk or on the phone. Please leave a message after the beep. I'll call you back as soon as I can. If you'd like to be connected with the receptionist, please press zero now, and someone will be right with you.

4. You've reached Grand Star. All of our lines are currently busy. Please hold, and your call will be answered shortly.

UNIT 3, EXERCISES 4 & 5, page 66

1. Hello. My name is Lahn Viet. That's V as in Victor/ I–E–T. I'm calling about the job as a carpenter's assistant. I saw your ad in the *Daily News*. My telephone number is 648-4792. Thank you. Goodbye.

2. Hello. This is Mohammed Abed. I worked in a hospital for a long time, but now I want to work in an office. Leilah Abed told me that you have a job opening. My number is 451-6324. Thank you.

3. Hello. My name is Ricardo Lopez. That's spelled L as in Lisa, O–P/E–Z as in Zebra. I'm interested in the job as a laboratory assistant. I saw your job listing at the University of Chicago. Thank you.

UNIT 3, EXERCISE 6, page 67

1. Applicant: Could I leave a message, please?
   Receptionist: Certainly. Could I have your name, please?
   Applicant: My name is Pablo Sananas.
   Receptionist: Could you spell your last name, please?
   Applicant: Sure. That's S–A–N as in Nancy.
   Receptionist: S–A–N.
   Applicant: A–N / A–S.
   Receptionist: A–N / A–S. S–A–N / A–N / A–S. Pablo Sananas.

2. Receptionist: Would you like to leave a message?
   Applicant: Yes. My name is Mary Kay Hunyady.
   Receptionist: Could you spell that, please?
   Applicant: Yes. H–U–N as in Nancy.
   Receptionist: H–U–N.
   Applicant: Y–A–D–Y.
   Receptionist: Y–A–D–Y. H–U–N / Y–A–D–Y, Hunyady.

3. Applicant: May I leave a message, please?
   Receptionist: Sure.
   Applicant: This is Ramiro Ochoa.
   Receptionist: Could you spell your last name, please?
   Applicant: Sure. That's spelled O–C–H / O–A.
   Receptionist: O–C–H / O–A. Ochoa.

4. Applicant: Could you take a message, please?
   Receptionist: Sure.
   Applicant: This is Nhu Vuong.
   Receptionist: Could you spell that, please?
   Applicant: Yes. That's V as in Victor U–O / N–G.
   Receptionist: V–U–O / N–G. Vuong.

UNIT 3, EXERCISE 16, page 72

1. Receptionist: Good morning, Columbia Company. How can I help you?
   Applicant: Hello, this is Raoul Garcia, and I'm calling about the job as a cashier. I saw your job listing at Ashley's Vocational Services. May I speak to Ms. Martin, please?
   Receptionist: Sure. Just a moment, please.

2. Receptionist: Fairway Hotel. May I help you?
   Applicant: Yes. This is Zoya Maklina. I'm interested in the job as a gardener. I saw your ad in the *Milwaukee Journal*. Could I speak to the person who does the hiring, please?
   Receptionist: Please hold. . . .

3. Receptionist: Tek Computers. Susan speaking. May I help you?

Applicant: Yes. This is Kin Phan. I'm calling about the job as a computer technician. Pedro Castillo told me you have a job opening. Could I speak to the personnel manager, please?
Receptionist: She's away from her desk.

4. Receptionist: Good afternoon. Precision Gears. How should I direct your call?
   Applicant: Hello. My name is Victor Leighton, and I'm calling about the job as a security guard. I saw your ad in the *Advertiser*. Could I talk to the person who does the hiring, please?
   Receptionist: I'll see if he's in.

5. Receptionist: Good afternoon. Realtime Video.
   Applicant: Hello. This is Camillo Matier. I'm interested in the job as a stock clerk. Sasha Robles told me you have a job opening. Could I speak to the person who does the hiring, please?
   Receptionist: I'm sorry. He's not in.

6. Receptionist: Fullerton Hospital. How may I direct your call?
   Applicant: Hello. This is Savannah Jackson. I'm interested in a job as a laboratory assistant. I saw your job listing at the State Employment Office. May I speak to the personnel manager, please?
   Receptionist: Just a minute. I'll connect you.

7. Receptionist: Good morning. Waterfront Restaurant.
   Applicant: Hello. My name is David Stern. I'm calling about a job as a busperson. Henry Bortman told me you have a job opening. Could I speak to Ms. Rudman, please?
   Receptionist: Well, she's in a meeting right now.

8. Receptionist: A-1 Bakery. Carol speaking. May I help you?
   Applicant: Hello. My name is Davida Corti, and I'm looking for a job as a bakery assistant. I saw your ad in the *Examiner*. Could I speak to the person who does the hiring, please?
   Receptionist: I'm sorry. She's not available.

UNIT 3, EXERCISES 19 & 20, page 75

1. Applicant: May I speak to Ms. Martin, please?
   Receptionist: Just a moment please. . . . I'm sorry. She's not in this morning.
   Applicant: Oh, she's out. Could you tell me when she will be available, please?
   Receptionist: Could you try again tomorrow before 11:00?
   Applicant: Sure. And could I leave a message, please?
   Receptionist: Yes.
   Applicant: Please tell her that Savannah Jackson called and that I'm very interested in the job as a cashier.
   Receptionist: That's Savannah Jackson, right?
   Applicant: Yes. My telephone number is 647-8926. I'm usually home in the afternoon.
   Receptionist: 647-8926. I'll tell Ms. Martin that you called.
   Applicant: Thank you.
   Receptionist: You're welcome. Goodbye.
   Applicant: Goodbye.

2. Applicant: Could I speak to the person who does the hiring, please?
   Receptionist: Just a moment, please, I'll see if he's in. . . . I'm sorry. He's not available right now. Could you call back later?
   Applicant: Yes, but may I have his name, please?

Receptionist: His name is Jose Arroyo.
Applicant: Um, could you tell me when he will be in, please?
Receptionist: Sure. He'll be in around 3:00.
Applicant: 3:00. I'll call back then. Thanks a lot.
Receptionist: You're welcome. Goodbye.
Applicant: Goodbye.

3. Applicant: Could I speak to the personnel manager, please?
Receptionist: She's in a meeting at the moment.
Applicant: Could you tell me her name, please?
Receptionist: Her name is Ellen Falconi.
Applicant: Ellen Fal . . . Could you spell the last name, please?
Receptionist: Sure. That's F–A–L–C as in Carol O–N–I.
Applicant: S–A–L.
Receptionist: No, that's F as in Frank.
Applicant: Oh, F–A–L / C–O–N–I?
Receptionist: That's correct.
Applicant: Thank you. And could I leave a message?
Receptionist: Yes. Go ahead.
Applicant: My name is Kin Phan. I'm calling about the job as a computer technician.
Receptionist: Okay. And what is your telephone number?
Applicant: 991-6766.
Receptionist: 991-6766. Okay. I'll give her the message.
Applicant: Thank you very much.
Receptionist: You're welcome. Goodbye.
Applicant: Goodbye.

UNIT 3, EXERCISE 21, page 75

1. Applicant: Could you tell me the manager's name, please?
Receptionist: Sure. Her name is Djuna Blagsvedt.
Applicant: Could you spell the last name, please?
Receptionist: Certainly. B–L–A / G as in George. . .
Applicant: B–L–A–G. . .
Receptionist: S–V–E / D as in David / T.
Applicant: S–V–E–D–T. Okay, so that's B–L–A–G / S–V / E–D–T?
Receptionist: Right.
Applicant: And is that Mr. or Ms.?
Receptionist: It's Ms. Blagsvedt.
Applicant: Thank you.

2. Applicant: Could you tell me his name, please?
Receptionist: Sure. His name is Oscar Hernandez.
Applicant: Could you spell the last name, please?
Receptionist: Sure. H–E–R as in Robert.
Applicant: H–E–R.
Receptionist: N–A–N.
Applicant: N–A–N.
Receptionist: D–E–Z.
Applicant: D–E–Z. H–E–R / N–A–N / D–E–Z. And, is that Mr. or Mrs.
Receptionist: It's Mr. Hernandez.
Applicant: Thank you.

3. Applicant: Could I have the manager's name, please?
Receptionist: Certainly. His name is Eric Kupferman.
Applicant: Could you spell the last name, please?
Receptionist: Yes. That's K–U–P / F as in Frank. . .
Applicant: K–U–P–F. . .
Receptionist: E–R / M–A–N.
Applicant: E–R / M–A–N. K–U–P / F–E–R / M–A–N.
Receptionist: That's correct.
Applicant: And is that Mr. of Ms.?
Receptionist: It's Mr. Kupferman.
Applicant: Thank you very much.

UNIT 3, EXERCISE 25, page 79

1. What is this regarding?
2. That position is filled.
3. How should I direct your call?
4. Who should I say is calling?
5. Could you call again tomorrow?
6. Who would you like to speak with?
7. We're no longer accepting applications.
8. Would you like to leave a message?

UNIT 4, EXERCISE 1, page 87

Receptionist: Good morning, Vogue Graphics. How can I help you?
Applicant: Hello, this is Carlos Paz, and I'm calling about the job as a copy machine operator. I saw your ad in the *Daily News*. Could I speak to Ms. Sudak, please?
Receptionist: Sure. Just a moment, please.
Manager: Hi. This is Linda Sudak. May I help you?
Applicant: Hello. This is Carlos Paz, and I'm calling about the job as a copy machine operator. I saw your ad in the *Daily News*. I was an office clerk in a large electronics company for three years, and I'm really interested in this job.

UNIT 4, EXERCISE 3, page 90

1. Applicant: Hi. This is Bing Fan. I'm calling about the job as a computer technician. I have two years' experience as a computer technician, and I know how to repair computers very well.
Manager: Could you tell me more about your experience?
Applicant: Well, in my last job, I installed, tested, and repaired computer equipment. I am a good problem solver, so it was easy for me to find the problems and repair the computers I worked on. I know how to fix mainframe and personal computers.

2. Applicant: Hello. My name is Karen Ashley, and I'm interested in a job as a baker's assistant. I saw your job listing at the State Employment Agency. I was a baker's assistant for four years. I've always loved to bake.
Manager: Can you tell me about your experience?
Applicant: I worked as a baker's assistant in a small bakery. In my last job, I helped the bakers with everything. I can make many kinds of bread, for example, French bread and wheat bread and all kinds of cookies. I know how to make special cakes for birthdays and weddings.

3. Applicant: Hello. This is Liz Fisher, and I'm calling about the job as a copy machine operator. I saw your ad in the *Tribune*. In my last job, I was an electrician. I'm very organized and efficient.
Manager: What can you tell me about your last job?
Applicant: In my last job, I fixed many kinds of machines and equipment. When I was an electrician, I fixed electronic equipment every day. I'm very good with my hands, and I'm also good with numbers.

4. Applicant: Hello. This is Sergey Markman. I'm looking for a job as a refrigeration repair person. My cousin, Irina Markman, told me you have a job opening now. In my last job, I was a manager in an appliance store. I'm very friendly and efficient.
Manager: Can you tell me a little more about your experience?
Applicant: I studied refrigerator repair at vocational school, and I have a certificate now. I know how to fix all different types of refrigerators. I'm good with my hands, and I'm very strong.

UNIT 4, EXERCISE 5, page 91

1. Manager: Can you tell me more about your experience?
   Applicant: When I was a baker's assistant in a small bakery for four years, I helped the bakers with everything. I can make many kinds of bread, for example, French bread and wheat bread and all kinds of cookies. And I know how to make special cakes for birthdays and weddings.

2. Manager: What can you tell me about your last job?
   Applicant: In my last job, I installed, tested, and repaired computer equipment. I am a good problem solver, so it was easy for me to find the problems and repair the computers I worked on. I know how to fix mainframe and personal computers. I'm studying at City College to learn about the newest computers now.

3. Manager: Can you tell me a little more about your experience?
   Applicant: When I was a manager, I worked with many different kinds of people, and I am friendly. When I came here, I studied refrigerator repair at vocational school, and I have a certificate now. I know how to fix all different types of refrigerators. I'm good with my hands, and I'm very strong.

UNIT 4, EXERCISES 11 & 12, page 95

1. Applicant: Hello. My name is Jim Kennedy. I'm interested in the job as an automobile body repair person. I came here with my family last month. There's my wife, three kids, and my mom. . . .
   Manager: Well, . . . what can you tell me about your experience?
   Applicant: [silence]
   Manager: Can you tell me about your experience?
   Applicant: Oh! Sure. In my last job, I worked in an automobile body repair shop. Ten people worked there, and we had a really good time. I worked from nine to five with an hour off for lunch every day. I got paid for holidays, vacations, and sick time. It was a great job.
   Manager: I see.

2. Applicant: Hello. My name is Alex Berdichevskiy. I'm calling about the job as a driver. My neighbor, Jody Sokolower, works for you, and she told me that you have a job opening.
   Manager: Uh-huh, do you have any experience as a taxi driver?
   Applicant: Yes. I have fifteen years' experience as a taxi driver.
   Manager: Well, tell me more about your driving experience. Where did you work?
   Applicant: Well, I drove six days a week when I worked in Moscow. And, let me think. I knew the fastest way to drive anywhere in the city. I knew all the little streets. I know how to get around this city, too. I drive everywhere so I can learn the streets.
   Manager: I see. Well, let me tell you what we're looking for.
   Applicant: Okay.
   Manager: We're looking for drivers *and* we're looking for dispatchers.
   Applicant: Excuse me. Could you explain the last part, please?
   Manager: Yes, dispatchers. Do you know how to use a taxi radio?
   Applicant: Oh, I see. Yes. I can use a radio.
   Manager: That's good.

Applicant: Well, could I make an appointment for an interview?

3. Applicant: Hello. This is Evelyn Chien. I'm a friend of Paulina Zurik. She told me that you have a job opening for a cosmetology assistant. I have ten years' experience as a cosmetologist.
   Manager: Excuse me. Could you repeat your name more slowly, please?
   Applicant: Oh, I'm sorry. My name is Evelyn Chien, and I'm calling about the job as a cosmetology assistant.
   Manager: All right, Evelyn. Can you tell me more about what you did?
   Applicant: Do you mean more about my experience?
   Manager: Yes, that's right.
   Applicant: Well, let me see. I worked in a hotel for two years, and then I had my own small beauty salon. There were two people working there, so I did everything.
   Manager: That's good.
   Applicant: I washed, cut, and styled hair. I also cleaned my salon. I really liked my last job because I talked to so many different people every day.
   Manager: Uh-huh.

UNIT 4, EXERCISE 13, page 95

1. Applicant: I wrote computer programs for schools, and I repaired computers. I studied computer repair at the university.
   Manager: Well, why don't you send me your resume?
   Applicant: Could I have your address, please?
   Manager: Sure.

2. Applicant: I set and cleared tables, made coffee, and helped the waiters and waitresses.
   Manager: Could you come in for an interview on Monday, August 14th?
   Applicant: That's fine.

3. Applicant: I had many different duties. For example, I answered the telephone, typed letters, and made copies. I liked my last job because I was busy and I'm very energetic.
   Manager: Could you fax me your resume today?
   Applicant: Yes.

4. Applicant: I used a cash register, counted money, and gave change. I am very good with numbers.
   Manager: I'm sorry. That position has been filled. Can you call back next month?
   Applicant: Certainly.

5. Applicant: I also cleaned my salon. I really liked my last job because I talked to so many different people every day.
   Manager: We're accepting applications all week between ten and five. Why don't you stop by sometime this week and fill out an application?

UNIT 4, EXERCISE 18, page 98

1. Manager: Well, why don't you send me your resume?
   Applicant: Could I have your address, please?
   Manager: Sure. It's eleven-seventeen Snelling Avenue.
   Applicant: That's eleven-seventy?
   Manager: No, one-one-one-seven.
   Applicant: Oh. 1–1–1–7. Could you spell the street, please?
   Manager: Sure. S–N as in Nancy, E–L–L / I–N–G.
   Applicant: S–N / E–L–L / I–N–G?
   Manager: Uh-huh.
   Applicant: Okay. Eleven-seventeen Snelling Avenue. And could you tell me the city, please?
   Manager: Sure. It's Saint Paul.

Applicant: Could you spell that, please?
Manager: Sure. S–A–I / N–T.
Applicant: S–A–I / N–T.
Manager: P–A–U–L.
Applicant: P–A–U–L. Saint Paul.
Manager: Right.
Applicant: And could I have your ZIP code?
Manager: 5–5–1–0–8.
Applicant: 5–5–1–0–8?
Manager: That's right.
Applicant: And who should I send my resume to?
Manager: You can send it to me. Steve Rodriguez.
Applicant: Could you spell your last name, please?
Manager: Sure. R–O–D as in David, R–I–G / U–E–Z.
Applicant: R–O–D, and then . . . ?
Manager: R–I–G.
Applicant: R–I–G.
Manager: U–E–Z.
Applicant: U–E–Z. Steve Rodriguez. Thank you. So that's eleven-seventeen Snelling Avenue, and your name is Steve Rodriguez.
Manager: That's right.
Applicant: I'll send my resume today. Thank you for your time.
Manager: You're welcome. Goodbye.
Applicant: Goodbye.

2. Manager: Would you like to come in and fill out an application?
Applicant: Sure. Could you tell me your address, please?
Manager: Fifty-two, twenty-five Alamo Street.
Applicant: Five-two-two-five?
Manager: Right.
Applicant: And could you spell the street, please?
Manager: Sure. That's A–L–A / M–O.
Applicant: A–L–A / M–O. So that's fifty-two, twenty-five Alamo Street.
Manager: Uh-huh.
Applicant: Could you tell me the cross streets, please?
Manager: 52nd and 53rd Avenue.
Applicant: 52nd and 51st Avenue?
Manager: No. That's 52nd and 53rd Avenue.
Applicant: Oh. 52nd and 53rd Avenue. And could you tell me your business hours, please?
Manager: We're open from eight to four. You can come in anytime Monday to Friday.
Applicant: Okay. And who should I ask for?
Manager: You can ask for me, Maraya.
Applicant: And could you spell your name, please?
Manager: M as in Mary A–R.
Applicant: M–A–R.
Manager: A–Y–A.
Applicant: A–Y–A. Maraya.
Manager: Uh-huh.
Applicant: Great! I'll come in this afternoon. Thanks a lot.
Manager: You're welcome. Goodbye.
Applicant: Goodbye.

3. Manager: Could you come in for an interview on Wednesday, July 5th?
Applicant: Sure. That's Wednesday. . .
Manager: Yes, Wednesday, July 5th.
Applicant: Okay, Wednesday, July 5th.
Manager: Is 9:30 convenient for you?
Applicant: Yes. 9:30 is fine. Could I have your address, please?
Manager: We're located at eight-oh-one First Street, Suite 200.
Applicant: That's eight-oh-one, and could you repeat the street, please?
Manager: First Street.
Applicant: That's 801 First Street, and could you repeat the last part, please?

Manager: Suite 200.
Applicant: Suite 200?
Manager: Right.
Applicant: So, that's 801 First Street, Suite 200.
Manager: Uh-huh.
Applicant: And could I have the cross streets, please?
Manager: We're between Main and Summit Street.
Applicant: I'm sorry. Could you repeat that, please?
Manager: Main and Summit.
Applicant: Could you spell the last street, please?
Manager: S–U–M / M–I–T.
Applicant: S–U–M / M–I–T. Main and Summit Streets. Okay, Mr. Johnson. I'll see you on Wednesday, July 5th at 9:30.
Manager: Right.
Applicant: Thank you. I look forward to meeting you.
Manager: I look forward to meeting you, too. Goodbye.
Applicant: Goodbye.

4. Manager: Could you come in for an interview on Tuesday, March 8th at 10:00?
Applicant: Sure, Thursday, March 8th at 10:00.
Manager: Not Thursday, *Tuesday*, March 8th.
Applicant: Oh, sure. Tuesday, March 8th at 10:00 is fine. Could you tell me the address, please?
Manager: Sixteen, ninety-six Jones Street.
Applicant: One-six-nine-six. And could you spell the street, please?
Manager: Sure. J as in John, O–N / E–S.
Applicant: J–O–N / E–S. Sixteen, ninety-six Jones Street.
Manager: Yes, that's right.
Applicant: Could you tell me the cross streets, please?
Manager: Spear Street and River Street.
Applicant: Could you spell the first street, please?
Manager: Sure. That's S–P–E / A–R.
Applicant: Okay. S–P–E / A–R. Spear Street. And could you repeat the other street, please?
Manager: River Street.
Applicant: Okay, Spear and River Street. So I'll see you on Tuesday, March 8th at 10:00. Thank you very much.
Manager: You're welcome. Goodbye.
Applicant: Goodbye.

UNIT 4, EXERCISE 20, page 100
Manager: Could you come in for an interview next week?
Applicant: Yes, that's fine.
Manager: How about next Tuesday, June 14th, at 10:00?
Applicant: Excuse me. Could you speak more slowly, please?
Manager: Certainly. Next Tuesday, June 14th at 10:00.
Applicant: Next Tuesday, June 14th, at 10:00?
Manager: Uh-huh.
Applicant: That's fine. Could I have your address, please?
Manager: Sure. It's forty-three, ninety-seven Oak Street, Suite 523.
Applicant: 4397 Oak Street. Could you repeat the last part, please?
Manager: Suite 523.
Applicant: Suite 523. I see. Could you tell me the cross streets, please?
Manager: We're between Park and Lakeshore.
Applicant: Okay. Between Park and Lakeshore?
Manager: Yes, that's right.
Applicant: And could I have your name, please?
Manager: My name is Alicia Bolanos.
Applicant: Could you spell your last name, please?
Manager: B–O–L / A–N as in Nancy / O–S.
Applicant: B–O–L / A–N / O–S?
Manager: Yes.
Applicant: Okay, Ms. Bolanos. I'll see you next Tuesday, June 14th, at 10:00. Thank you very much.
Manager: You're welcome. Goodbye.
Applicant: Goodbye.

UNIT 5, EXERCISE 1, page 105

1. I look for complete applications. It's important to answer all the questions. For example, if someone doesn't fill out dates and numbers, or an address, I think that person is not good with details, and I will not hire that person. I need workers who will complete every detail of the job and who know how to follow instructions.

2. Sometimes I get applications that I can't read because of the handwriting. People write in so many different ways, and some people's handwriting is impossible to read! I think job applicants should always print or type their applications. And please use a pen, not a pencil. The information is really important. After all, I can't call an applicant if I can't read the name.

3. I agree with Lilya. I think people should print. But I want to add that they should print *neatly* and *clearly*. People need to be careful when they fill out their applications. I mean, they shouldn't cross out words, and I really don't like spelling mistakes. If someone makes a mistake, then that person should ask for a new application or correct the mistakes very, *very* carefully.

UNIT 6, EXERCISE 12, page 139

Ashaki:	Hello?
Nehanda:	Hi, Ashaki. This is Nehanda. How are you?
Ashaki:	Fine, thanks. And you?
Nehanda:	Pretty good. I'm looking for a job as a hospital orderly, and I'm filling out job applications. Can I ask you a favor?
Ashaki:	Sure.
Nehanda:	Could I use your name as a reference?
Ashaki:	I'd be happy to be a personal reference.
Nehanda:	Thank you. Let's see. Could I check the spelling of your last name? Is it B–A–K / A–R–I?
Ashaki:	That's right.
Nehanda:	And, may I have your address, please?
Ashaki:	2830 College Avenue.
Nehanda:	2830 College Avenue?
Ashaki:	Right.
Nehanda:	Thanks a lot, Ashaki.
Ashaki:	You're welcome. And good luck!
Nehanda:	Thanks. Goodbye.
Ashaki:	Goodbye.

UNIT 7, EXERCISE 1, page 158

1. I think you need to do your homework before an interview. I mean, many interviewers ask the same questions. You should practice your answers to these questions. When applicants can't answer simple questions, they don't sound confident and they don't make a good impression.

2. Well, I think you should learn a little bit about the company and the job before you come to an interview. Then you seem really interested in the job. And know something about the job duties and the salary. Honestly, I've met with some people who didn't know anything about the job, or even the name of the company!

3. I think it's very important to come on time. Actually, it's better to come ten or fifteen minutes early just to be sure. I've never hired anyone who came late to an interview. I want my employees to be on time. And, if you bring a child or a friend . . . well then, it's hard to have a serious interview, don't you think?

4. Make sure that you know the right place, and that you come on the right day. For example, once somebody came on a *Tuesday* and the interview was scheduled for *Thursday*. I was busy and I couldn't meet with the person. And sometimes people don't know my name. I don't like that. You need to check these things. Really, you can't be disorganized.

5. What's important? Let's see . . . Well, sometimes you need to fill out an application right before the interview. So, you need all the information about your work history and your education—dates, addresses, job duties, things like that. And I like to see a list of references. It's a good idea to bring your resume, too.

6. Okay . . . how to prepare . . . You need to look professional. Your appearance is very important. Choose your interview clothes when you first start to look for a job—really early. Don't wait. The night before the interview is a bad time to think about what you will wear. And, of course, make sure everything is neat and clean—your clothes, your hair, your shoes.

UNIT 7, EXERCISE 3, page 160

1. I don't really want to hear about your personal problems or your life in general. I mean, what's happening with your husband, your wife, or your family—any of that. I'm an interviewer, not a friend. This is a business conversation. I just want to know if you're the best person for the job. I want to hear about your past jobs, your skills, and your qualities.

2. You need to answer questions completely. Give examples. If someone tells me she worked as a salesperson, I want to know what she did. Did she collect money? Did she put away clothes? Did she talk to customers? If someone says he is flexible, I want more information. Can he work any schedule? Can he change duties easily? When I'm deciding who to hire, I remember the applicants who gave examples.

3. I like good listeners. I mean, people who show me that they're really listening to what I say. An interview should be a conversation. Some people are completely silent, and I have no idea if they understand me or not. Be an active listener. For example, say something like, "I see," or "Uh-huh" if you understand. And ask questions when you don't understand, or if I'm talking too fast. I'm happy to repeat myself or explain something.

4. Of course, most people are nervous when they go to a job interview, but you need to be confident. When you meet an interviewer, shake hands and make eye contact. If someone doesn't look at me, it makes me feel uncomfortable. During the interview, try not to move your hands or feet nervously. Sit up straight. And, let's see. Make sure I can hear you. Don't speak too softly. I need confident people on the job, so show me that you're confident during the interview.

5. Sometimes I interview ten to twenty people for one job, so you really need to sell yourself in an interview. I like people who are positive. You need to be positive about what you can do. Then I'll think that you really want the job and that you'll work hard. Say good things about yourself. Never say bad things about a past manager or a past job. And, you know, positive people are more fun to work with. They get along better with their co-workers.

UNIT 7, EXERCISE 5, page 161

Interviewer:	Could you tell me a little about your background?
Applicant:	Excuse me. Could you say that in another way?
Interviewer:	Sure. Tell me something about yourself. Where are you from? What kind of work did you do?
Applicant:	I see. Well, I'm from Mexico. I came here six months ago. In Mexico, I was a mechanic for five years.
Interviewer:	Okay, good. Let me see, could you tell me a little more about your experience? What kind of tools do you know how to use? What do you know about American cars?
Applicant:	I'm sorry. Could you speak more slowly, please?
Interviewer:	Oh, sorry. Tell me about your experience. What kind of tools can you use? What do you know about American cars?

Applicant: Let me think. In my last job, I worked on many different kinds of cars. Sometimes I worked on American cars. And the tools are the same in my country.

Interviewer: Okay. Well, this is a part-time, temporary position. Does that sound okay to you?

Applicant: I think so. I understand that this is a part-time job, but what does "temporary" mean?

Interviewer: Well, this job will not last for a long time. It's a three-month job.

Applicant: Okay, I see. That's fine with me.

UNIT 7, EXERCISE 10, page 163

Receptionist: Good morning. May I help you?

Applicant: Hello. My name is Doug Marcus. I have an interview with Julie Wang at ten o'clock.

Receptionist: Could you have a seat, please? I'll tell her that you are here.

Applicant: Thank you.

Interviewer: Hello. My name is Julie Wang.

Applicant: Hello. My name is Doug Marcus. It's nice to meet you.

Interviewer: It's nice to meet you, too.

UNIT 7, EXERCISE 13, page 166

1. What shift can you work?
2. Are you interested in part-time or full-time work?
3. What salary would you like to earn?
4. This is a temporary job. Is that okay for you?
5. What date are you available?
6. Are you currently employed?
7. Could I contact your supervisor?
8. What kind of work are you looking for?
9. What experience do you have for this position?
10. Could you give me some references?

UNIT 7, EXERCISES 16 & 17, page 172

1. When can you start?
2. Are you working now?
3. Do you want to work part-time or full-time?
4. Where did you work?
5. Are you interested in permanent or temporary work?
6. Do you have a list of your references?
7. What hours can you work?
8. The salary is $7.00 an hour. Is that okay with you?

UNIT 7, EXERCISE 19, page 174

1. Interviewer: Hi. Hadid Arana? I'm Eduardo Rodriguez. Nice to meet you.

   Applicant: Nice to meet you, too.

   Interviewer: So, Mr. Arana. You're applying for a job as a security guard, right?

   Applicant: Yes.

   Interviewer: Are you working now?

   Applicant: Yes, I have a part-time job in a restaurant during the day, but I want to work at night.

   Interviewer: Good. I'd like to tell you about the job. The schedule is Monday through Friday. . . .

   Applicant: Okay, Monday to Friday . . .

   Interviewer: And the hours are from 10:00 P.M. to 7:00 A.M. Is that okay with you?

   Applicant: Uh-huh . . . 10:00 P.M. to 7:00 A.M.

   Interviewer: Yes.

   Applicant: Yes, that's fine.

   Interviewer: It's a full-time position, forty hours a week, but the position is temporary, for three months.

   Applicant: Excuse me. Could you say that a little slower, please?

   Interviewer: Sure. The position is full-time, forty hours a week.

   Applicant: Oh, good. It's full-time.

   Interviewer: Yes. And it's a temporary position. The job ends on July 30th.

Applicant: Oh, I see. So the job is finished at the end of July.

Interviewer: That's right. The salary is $7.00 an hour. Are you interested?

Applicant: Yes. It sounds great.

Interviewer: Well, the job starts this Monday, May 2nd. Can you start then?

Applicant: Let's see. Monday, May 2nd . . . Yes, I can.

Interviewer: And do you have a list of your references?

Applicant: Yes, here you are.

Interviewer: Thank you. I want to call your references, and I'll call you on Thursday.

Applicant: Thank you for your time.

Interviewer: You're welcome.

Applicant: Goodbye.

Interviewer: Goodbye.

2. Interviewer: Hello, Renate Chopard? My name is Mahasen Ajlan. Have a seat, please.

   Applicant: Thank you. It's nice to meet you, Ms. Ajlan.

   Interviewer: It's nice to meet you, too. So, what position are you applying for?

   Applicant: I'm applying for a job as a health club attendant.

   Interviewer: Uh-huh. Have you worked in a health club before?

   Applicant: No, I haven't, but I've worked as a housekeeper for many years, and I'm very neat and organized.

   Interviewer: Sounds good. Well, let me tell you a little about the position. It's part-time, and the hours are 6:00 A.M. to 11:00 A.M. Are you available then?

   Applicant: I see. Part-time is fine, and six to eleven is no problem. I like to get up early in the morning.

   Interviewer: And it's five days a week, Wednesday through Sunday. Is that okay?

   Applicant: Yes, Wednesday to Sunday is fine.

   Interviewer: All right. I see on your application that you're from Switzerland. Do you have a green card, a passport, or other proof of your employment eligibility?

   Applicant: Yes, I do. Here you are.

   Interviewer: Thank you. And let's see . . . what salary do you hope to earn?

   Applicant: I've heard that the usual salary is from $6.00 to $9.00 an hour.

   Interviewer: Well, most of our attendants start at $6.00 an hour. How's that?

   Applicant: $6.00. That's fine.

   Interviewer: Good. Are you working now?

   Applicant: No, I'm not. I just arrived here six weeks ago.

   Interviewer: So, when can you start?

   Applicant: Anytime.

   Interviewer: How about this Thursday?

   Applicant: That sounds great!

   Interviewer: You start at 6:00 A.M., July 24th.

   Applicant: Okay. That's Thursday, July 24th at 6:00 A.M.

   Interviewer: Right. Be sure to come on time.

   Applicant: I will. Thanks a lot. I'm really looking forward to working here.

   Interviewer: We're happy to have you. Goodbye.

   Applicant: Goodbye.

UNIT 8, EXERCISES 1 & 2, page 179

1. Interviewer: When you interview job applicants, what information do you want to find out?

   Manager: I really want to get to know the people I interview.

   Interviewer: What do you mean?

   Manager: Well, I want to find out more about their personalities.

Interviewer: Oh, their personal qualities.
Manager: Yes. Are they confident? Are they flexible? Are they friendly?
Interviewer: Uh-huh.
Manager: I want to know if they will work well with the people in our company, and if the people in our company will like working with them.
Interviewer: I see. So you're saying that you want to hire people who will fit into the company.
Manager: That's right.

2. Interviewer: What do you look for when you interview job applicants?
Manager: Well, I want to know if applicants are really interested in the job. Are they enthusiastic? If applicants show me that they really want the job and are enthusiastic, then I think they will work hard.
Interviewer: Okay. So you want to hire people who are enthusiastic about the job they're applying for.
Manager: Right. And they need to have clear goals for the future.
Interviewer: Uh-huh.
Manager: I like to hire applicants who will stay with the company. I don't want to hire people who will leave after a few months. After all, we spend a lot of time and money training new employees.
Interviewer: So, you want to find people who will stay with your company. Good point.

3. Interviewer: When you interview job applicants, what kind of information are you interested in finding out?
Manager: I want to know more about applicants' skills and experience. I already know something about that from the resume. . . .
Interviewer: Right.
Manager: But can they really do the job they're applying for? I mean, do they have the skills they need for the job?
Interviewer: Okay.
Manager: I need details about applicants' skills.
Interviewer: What kind of details?
Manager: What do they know how to do? For example, can they use a computer? What kinds of computer programs can they use, that sort of thing.
Interviewer: I see. Do you want to find out anything else?
Manager: Yes, I need concrete examples from their experience. What were their past job duties?
Interviewer: Uh-huh.
Manager: And, in fact, I usually have a lot of applicants with good skills and experience. That's why other things are important, too.
Interviewer: I see. Skills and experience *are* important, but you want to find out more.
Manager: That's correct.

UNIT 8, EXERCISES 6 & 7, page 182

1. Interviewer: Can you tell me about your background?
Applicant: I worked as a lab assistant in my country. It's a boring job, but I'm good at it.

2. Interviewer: Tell me about yourself.
Applicant: I'm from the Cambodia. Now I'd like to work as a nurse's assistant. In my last job, I was a nurse. I worked in a hospital emergency room. I have a lot of experience working in hospitals.

3. Interviewer: Could you tell me a little about your background?
Applicant: Now I would like to work as a cashier. I worked as a postal clerk in a small post office in China for six years. I know how to collect money and give change. I'm very good with numbers.

4. Interviewer: Can you tell me a little about yourself?
Applicant: I came here with my family five months ago. I have a wonderful wife and three children. My son is very good at sports, like me, and my wife is looking for a job, too. I'd like to work as a health club attendant.

5. Interviewer: Can you tell me a little bit about yourself?
Applicant: I'm from Eritrea. Right now I'd like to work as a photo lab assistant. I was a student in my country, and I want to study here at night and work during the day. I took several photography classes at the university, and I learned how to use photo lab equipment.

UNIT 8, EXERCISE 10, page 183

1. Interviewer: What were your major responsibilities in your last job?
Applicant: I'm sorry. Could you say that in another way, please?
Interviewer: Sure. Tell me what you did in your last job. What kind of experience do you have?
Applicant: Oh. I was a dentist for five years. My father and grandfather were dentists, too. I worked with my father in his office. The people in the office were nice.

2. Interviewer: What duties from your last job will help you as a cashier?
Applicant: In my last job, I helped customers at the post office. I answered their questions. I mailed their letters and packages, and gave them stamps. I collected money and gave them change. My job duties were similar to a cashier's duties.

3. Interviewer: Tell me about your experience.
Applicant: As I said, after I finished school, I worked as a hotel clerk. I gave keys to the guests and showed them their rooms. I liked working in a hotel because I really enjoy meeting different kinds of people. I liked talking to them and answering their questions. After that, I worked as a soccer coach in a high school for three years. I helped my students improve their soccer skills. I love sports. That's why I want to work in a health club.

4. Interviewer: Can you tell me about your last job?
Applicant: I was a lab assistant in my last job. I worked in the same company for seven years. I want to do the same work in this country.

5. Interviewer: What were your main duties in your last job?
Applicant: Excuse me . . . My last job . . . and could you repeat the first part, please?
Interviewer: Sure. What were your main duties? What did you do at your job every day?
Applicant: As I said, I have a lot of experience. First, I worked as a nurse in a big city clinic for three years. I worked with children. I took their temperatures, gave them medicines, and I also helped the doctors. After that, I worked at a hospital in the emergency room. I had many of the same duties in that job.

UNIT 8, EXERCISE 17, page 187

1. Interviewer: What are your greatest strengths?
   Applicant: I'm very energetic and love to be active. In my last job, I was a dancer.
   Interviewer: I see.
   Applicant: A dancer needs to have a lot of energy to dance and rehearse all day, and I know health club attendants need to be energetic, too.
   Interviewer: That's right. You need to be on your feet all day.
   Applicant: Uh-huh. And I really love sports, and I love talking to people about exercise and health. I know health club attendants need to be friendly and answer questions, and I'm very friendly. That's why I think I'm the best person for this position.

2. Interviewer: So you want to be an auto body repair person.
   Applicant: Yes.
   Interviewer: Tell me, why should I hire you for this position?
   Applicant: I'm really good with my hands, and I'm very careful with details. In my last job, I worked in a furniture factory, and I put furniture together. I worked very quickly and very carefully.
   Interviewer: Okay.
   Applicant: And I know a lot about cars. When I was young, my father always worked on cars at our house. I often helped him, and I learned a lot from him.
   Interviewer: Oh, good. That's good.
   Applicant: And I still like to work on cars. My hobby is buying old cars, fixing them, and selling them.
   Interviewer: Great!

3. Interviewer: Ten people applied for this job as a warehouse worker. Why should I hire you?
   Applicant: That's a hard question. Let me think. Well, I've never worked as a warehouse worker before, but I'm a fast learner, and I think I can do this job.
   Interviewer: Uh-huh.
   Applicant: And I'm a very hard worker . . . and, let me think . . . oh, and I'm very strong.

4. Interviewer : What are your greatest strengths?
   Applicant: Well, I have some experience as a cashier. I'm pretty good at math. I don't make a lot of mistakes.
   Interviewer: Uh-huh.
   Applicant: Also, I'm efficient. I mean, I'm very organized.
   Interviewer: All right. Anything else?
   Applicant: Oh, yes. I also work well with people. I'm really interested in this position. I think I can do a good job.

5. Interviewer: What are your best work abilities and personal qualities?
   Applicant: In my last job as a waiter, my schedule changed very often, but that was okay for me because I'm very flexible.
   Interviewer: Uh-huh.
   Applicant: If the schedule changes in your restaurant, I can be flexible here, too. And I was always on time for work. My boss knew that I was reliable.
   Interviewer: That's very important here. The last busperson was always late, so I had to fire her.
   Applicant: Well, you don't have to worry about me. I won't be late!

Interviewer: That's good.
Applicant: And, as I said, I was a waiter, so I know that a waiter and a busperson need to work well together.
Interviewer: Yes, that's true.
Applicant: And I really know the job. Sometimes we had 100 customers in our restaurant in one night. I helped the busperson clean the tables very quickly so new customers could sit down.

UNIT 8, EXERCISE 18, page 187

1. Interviewer: What are your greatest strengths?
   Applicant: I'm very energetic and love to be active. In my last job, I was a dancer.
   Interviewer: I see.
   Applicant: A dancer needs to have a lot of energy to dance and rehearse all day, and I know health club attendants need to be energetic, too.
   Interviewer: That's right. You need to be on your feet all day.
   Applicant: Uh-huh. And I really love sports, and I love talking to people about exercise and health. I know health club attendants need to be friendly and answer questions, and I'm very friendly. That's why I think I'm the best person for this position.

2. Interviewer: So you want to be an auto body repair person.
   Applicant: Yes.
   Interviewer: Tell me, why should I hire you for this position?
   Applicant: I'm really good with my hands, and I'm very careful with details. In my last job, I worked in a furniture factory, and I put furniture together. I worked very quickly and very carefully.
   Interviewer: Okay.
   Applicant: And I know a lot about cars. When I was young, my father always worked on cars at our house. I often helped him, and I learned a lot from him.
   Interviewer: Oh, good. That's good.
   Applicant: And I still like to work on cars. My hobby is buying old cars, fixing them and selling them.
   Interviewer: Great!

3. Interviewer: What are your best work abilities and personal qualities?
   Applicant: In my last job as a waiter, my schedule changed very often, but that was okay for me because I'm very flexible.
   Interviewer: Uh-huh.
   Applicant: If the schedule changes in your restaurant, I can be flexible here, too. And I was always on time for work. My boss knew that I was reliable.
   Interviewer: That's very important here. The last busperson was always late, so I had to fire her.
   Applicant: Well, you don't have to worry about me. I won't be late!
   Interviewer: That's good.
   Applicant: And, as I said, I was a waiter, so I know that a waiter and a busperson need to work well together.
   Interviewer: Yes, that's true.
   Applicant: And I really know the job. Sometimes we had 100 customers in our restaurant in one night. I helped the busperson clean the tables very quickly so new customers could sit down.

UNIT 8, EXERCISES 29 & 30, page 193

1. Interviewer: What's your weakest point?
   Applicant: I worked in a photo lab before, but I never used the equipment that you have in your company. I'm a fast learner, and I'm very good with my hands. I love learning how to use new machines, and I know a lot about photography. I'm sure I'll be able to use the equipment here very soon.

2. Interviewer: What is your weakest point? Do you think language will be a problem?
   Applicant: Yes, it's a problem for me. I'm afraid my English is not good enough.
   Interviewer: Uh-huh . . .
   Applicant: I can't understand people. They talk fast.
   Interviewer: Well, you know a waitress needs to talk to customers and co-workers.
   Applicant: Oh, yes. I'm a very good waitress. I have six years' experience.
   Interviewer: Uh-huh . . .

3. Interviewer: What's your biggest weakness?
   Applicant: Well, I've never thought about that. I can't really think of any weaknesses right now.
   Interviewer: Isn't there anything in your work that you think you need to improve?
   Applicant: Well, it was difficult for me to get to work on time in my last job.

4. Interviewer: What's your weakest point?
   Applicant: I've never worked in a child care center, but I worked as a children's nurse in my country, so I know how to take care of children. Right now I'm taking classes in early childhood development, and I'm learning a lot about teaching young children. I love working with children, and I think I will be a very good teacher's assistant.

5. Interviewer: What part of your work needs the most improvement?
   Applicant: Well, some people say I'm too friendly. When I worked as a salesclerk, I talked to the customers a lot. Sometimes I needed to stay late to put away all the clothes, but the customers were happy because I answered their questions. Then I started to use my time more efficiently. I put away the clothes when business was slow, and I finished my work on time. I'm always trying to do my job better.

UNIT 8, EXERCISES 33 & 34, page 195

1. Interviewer: What are your career goals?
   Applicant: Excuse me. Could you repeat the last word, please?
   Interviewer: *Goals*, your career goals.
   Applicant: Oh, I see. Right now I would like to be a lab assistant. At the same time, I want to study English and improve my computer skills. In say, three years, I want to have my laboratory technologist license. I would like to stay with your hospital and move up to a lab technologist position if possible.

2. Interviewer: What are your career goals?
   Applicant: Right now, I'd like to work as a stock clerk, but in the future, I plan to be a computer programmer.
   Interviewer: Well, that's very different, isn't it?
   Applicant: Yes, but I'm going to study programming for a few years, and I want to work here and study at the same time.
   Interviewer: So, you don't want to move up in our company, then?

Applicant: Well, I'm really not sure right now. But I really want to work here for two or three years. As you said, the schedule is flexible, and that's very important to me. I'm friendly and organized, and I'm a very hard worker. I know I'm a good person for this job!

3. Interviewer: So, you're applying for a position as a maintenance worker.
   Applicant: Yes.
   Interviewer: What are your plans for the future?
   Applicant: I'm going to be a film director.
   Interviewer: Oh, really. That's interesting! How do you plan to do that?
   Applicant: I don't know, but film directors make a lot of money, and it's an exciting job!
   Interviewer: I see. Well, how long do you plan to stay with this company, then?
   Applicant: Maybe a few months. I don't know if I'll like the job.

4. Interviewer: What direction do you see yourself going in?
   Applicant: Excuse me. Could you say that in another way, please?
   Interviewer: Sure. What are your plans for the future?
   Applicant: As I said, I have over ten years' experience working in restaurants, and I enjoy that kind of work. I'd like to become a waiter in the future. I think that a job as a busperson is a good place to start and a good way to learn about your restaurant.
   Interviewer: I think so, too.
   Applicant: I would like to know about how things work here, and I want to get to know the customers because I'd like to work here for a long time. I plan to study English and work hard.

5. Interviewer: What kind of future do you see for yourself?
   Applicant: I'd like to be a cashier.
   Interviewer: Okay, I understand that you want to be a cashier now, but what do you want to do in two or three years from now?
   Applicant: Well, I really want to work as a cashier in the future, too. I enjoy people. I'd like to learn more about your products and the customers who come here.
   Interviewer: That's good.
   Applicant: I'm very enthusiastic, and I'm sure the customers will like me.
   Interviewer: Uh-huh.
   Applicant: I would like to work here for a long time.

UNIT 8, EXERCISE 39, page 198

1. Can you tell me about your experience?
2. What are your strongest points?
3. What would you like to be doing in three years?
4. What are your greatest strengths?
5. What is your weakest point?
6. Could you tell me about your background?
7. What salary are you looking for?
8. What is your biggest weakness?
9. What are your plans for the future?
10. Could you tell me about yourself?

UNIT 8, EXERCISE 42, page 202

Interviewer: Thank you for coming in.
Applicant: It was very nice to meet you.
Interviewer: It was nice to meet you, too.
Applicant: When do you think you will make a decision?
Interviewer: Well, probably next Thursday or Friday.
Applicant: Okay. Should I contact you or will you contact me?
Interviewer: I'll contact you.
Applicant: Thank you.
Interviewer: You're welcome.
Applicant: Goodbye.
Interviewer: Goodbye.